Motoring
in Europe

C000259016

The essential handbook for the independent motorist abroad

This guide has been produced to assist motorists to have enjoyable, worry free motoring when taking UK registered vehicles to Continental Europe or the Republic of Ireland. It provides information about those most popular destination countries covered by RAC's Standard European Motoring Assistance. The remaining countries west of the Urals plus Turkey are also included and these, together with 'Standard' countries, are covered by RAC's Additional European Motoring Assistance.

Whenever you are travelling we strongly recommend you have the protection of RAC European Motoring Assistance, call free 0800 55 00 55 for details. Please also ensure you are aware of the motoring requirements and regulations for all the countries you are visiting. Contact RAC Travel Information on 0891 347 333* for the latest information.

Bon voyage.

*0891 numbers are charged at 60p per minute at all times. Calls from mobile phones may cost more. Information correct at May 1999.

Compiled by Travel Research Unit, RAC Motoring Services Ltd., Great Park Road, Bradley Stoke, Bristol BS32 4QN. Published by West One (Trade) Publishing Ltd, Portland House, 4 Great Portland Street, London W1N 5AA. Tel: 0171 580 6886.

© RAC Motoring Services Ltd. 1999.

ISBN 1 900327 41 4

Printed and bound in Italy

Contents

Documents

Before a journey, allow plenty of time to arrange for the preparation of all necessary documents – passports, visas, driving licences, insurances and vaccinations.

RAC will give advice on what documents are required for which countries; remember to ask about countries visited in transit as well as your destination country.

The following information applies only to British Subjects holding, or entitled to, a Foreign Office passport bearing the inscription 'United Kingdom of Great Britain and Northern Ireland'. Non-British citizens travelling in Europe should apply to their Embassy, Consulate or High Commission for information if in doubt.

Passports

Although continental European countries have abandoned routine passport checks at land frontiers, visitors are still expected to be able to provide proof of identity by way of a valid passport or identity card while in their country. It is a legal obligation in certain countries to carry such a document at all times. In addition, carrying a passport will help airline and ferry companies with passenger checks, obtaining assistance from British consular posts; hotel registration; banking services; and when returning to UK at immigration controls.

Each person in the party must hold, or be named on, a current passport valid for the countries of visit. Children under 16 must hold their own passports. However, those already included in a passport may continue to travel on it while it remains valid, until they reach 16 years.

The issue of 'family passports' including the particulars of wife/husband has been discontinued, however existing documents issued may continue to be used until expiry.

A UK passport of 32 pages costs £21 (children under 16 years £11) and 48 pages costs £31. Both are valid for 10 years.

Two photographs, of not more than 45mm by 35mm (1.77in x 1.38in), are required. One of these photographs should be signed on the reverse by a doctor, lawyer, MP or person of similar standing who has known the applicant for more than two years.

The passport application form should also be countersigned by the same person.

Passport application forms are available from main post offices. Completed forms, the fee, photographs and appropriate enclosures should be returned to a regional Passport Office, determined by your home address, for processing. The addresses of the Passport Offices are given on the application form. Passport Office hours of business are Mon–Fri 0900–1630hrs, except the London office (open to personal callers only) which opens at 0815 and closes at 1600hrs. Applications should be sent at least one month before the passport is needed. The peak period for passport applications is Jan-July so it is advisable to apply in the autumn if a new passport is required for the following year. Passport Agency information line Tel: 0870 521 0410.

Motor Insurance

International Motor Insurance Certificate (Green Card)

Motor vehicle insurance for minimum Third Party risks is compulsory in Europe.

This is provided by most UK and Eire policies covering all EU countries and certain other European countries.

Unless your insurer is notified that you are travelling in Europe, your Comprehensive Insurance may be automatically reduced to Third Party Cover.

The Green Card provides additional evidence that third party cover is held but it is not a legal requirement. Contact your insurers for advice.

A Green Card is compulsory in Andorra.

A Green Card is strongly recommended for travel in Spain, Portugal, Italy, Hungary and Greece. Your Green Card should be valid for both the European and Asian sectors when travelling in Turkey. In Bulgaria, Poland and Romania visiting motorists without a Green Card must take out short term insurance at the border on arrival. Lithuania is not part of the Green Card system and short term insurance must be arranged at the border.

When taking a caravan abroad, you should check with your insurance company that your policy covers towing a caravan in Europe as you may have to pay an extra premium.

Driving Licences

A valid, full driving licence should be carried by all motorists in Europe. Most European countries recognise a UK driving licence, although reference should be made to the introduction in the Europe by Country section of this guide.

An International Driving Permit (IDP) is normally required in those countries where a UK licence is not recognised.

Valid for one year, this is an internationally recognised document available for drivers holding a valid, full licence and aged 18 or over.

The IDP currently costs £4.00 and application forms are available from RAC Travel Services, Tel: 0800 55 00 55. A passport-size photograph is required, in addition to a current driving licence.

In Europe people under 18 are not normally permitted to drive. (Warning: European car hire companies may restrict drivers under 21 or even under 25.)

Your driving licence should be carried with you as it must be produced at once, on demand; there is no discretionary period as in the UK.

Holders of 'green' style licences may exchange these licences for an EC format 'pink/green' licence on completion of the D1 application form available from main post offices. A fee of £6.00 should accompany the application to DVLA, Swansea.

Holders of non-UK licences requiring an IDP, must apply to the relevant licensing authority or motoring organisation in the country in which the licence was issued.

Vehicle Registration Documents

A vehicle registration document must be carried when driving a UK-registered vehicle abroad. If the document is in the process of being replaced at the time you are travelling, you can apply for a Certificate of Registration (V379). You can do this at your local Vehicle Registration Office (VRO).

The address of your nearest office can be obtained by contacting DVLA on Tel: 01792 772134.

This is internationally recognised in lieu of the registration document and should be carried with you.

Should the vehicle not be registered in your name, eg if it is a company car, written authority for you to use it should be obtained from its owner.

If this is the case and you are travelling in Portugal, a special form of authority should be used and this can be obtained from RAC.

Taking a hired or leased vehicle abroad requires a Vehicle on Hire/Lease Certificate (VE 103) as the vehicle registration document is held by the hire/leasing company and this can be obtained from RAC Travel Services Tel: 0800 55 00 55.

Loss of Documents

Should any of the above documents be lost or stolen, immediately notify the nearest police station; inform RAC and the National Club of the country concerned.

Foreign Customs can enforce payment of duty in lieu of evidence of export if your vehicle is stolen or destroyed by fire. Indemnity covering this is provided for under RAC European Motoring Assistance providing that reasonable security measures have been taken.

Medical requirements

A useful booklet entitled "Health Advice for Travellers" (ref.T6) is available from post offices and by telephoning the Health Literature Line (Tel: 0800 55 57 77) at any time. The line is free of charge.
Free or reduced cost emergency treatment is available in the European Economic Area (EEA) countries on production of form E111 found in the above booklet which must be counter-signed by the post office before use.
However, travellers should note that cover under this scheme is minimal and it is strongly recommended to arrange additional travel insurance such as RAC European Personal Travel Insurance.
For details Tel: 0800 55 00 55.

Essential accessories

RAC Travel Centres can supply accessories which are legally required, useful or helpful when travelling in Europe. They are also available by telephone from RAC Travel Services on 0800 55 00 55.

Headlamps

Headlamp beams should be adjusted before driving on the right. Headlamp beam benders or reflectors make this an easy task as they alter the direction of the beam when stuck to the glass. Don't forget to remove them on returning to the UK.
Carry spare bulbs of the correct wattage for your lights as they may be difficult to obtain abroad. In Spain and certain other countries it is compulsory to carry a spare set of bulbs.

Snow Chains

Snow chains are a legal requirement during the winter when travelling in alpine countries.
They are available from RAC for purchase or hire and cover most makes of car.
Further details from RAC Travel Services (Tel: 0800 55 00 55) or they can be collected from the RAC Travel Centres in Dover and Portsmouth.

Where to Position the Warning Triangle

Warning triangles must be placed on the road at the rear of a vehicle (not a motorcycle) which has broken down on an open road at night, in poor visibility during the day, or on a bend in the road or on a hill.
Different countries have different regulations as to how far away from the car the warning triangle should be placed if you need to use it.
The specific country requirements can be found on the casing of the RAC Warning Triangle (and on other leading brands).

Tachograph

A tachograph is an essential fitment to all UK-registered vehicles travelling in the EU, which are constructed and equipped to carry ten or more people, including the driver.
Please refer to your local Department of Transport Traffic Area Office for further information.

Preparing your car

Even well-maintained cars can break down without any warning, but some simple preventive maintenance before you contemplate a long journey can minimise the chances of an unexpected road-side stop.
The main causes of breakdowns are the ignition/electrical system closely followed by the fuel and cooling systems. Preventive maintenance and inspection prior to your journey is quite a simple task and can help avoid the inconvenience and worry associated with a breakdown.
Mechanical faults however are another matter, and when a major one occurs – either in the engine, gearbox or axle – a road-side repair is usually not practicable.

Battery

The main problems with the battery are usually associated with the two electrical connections to the battery terminals.
When corrosion occurs, the green or white powder fungus growing on the terminal can prevent power getting from the battery to the starter motor.
Even though the connections may appear clean on the exterior, it is advisable to remove the terminal connector* and to clean the contact surfaces with a wire brush or emery paper.
In order to prevent recurrence of corrosion, apply a smear of petroleum jelly to the connections before they are re-made and again afterwards to cover all outermost surfaces of the connector and battery terminal. Another common cause for the starter motor not working, apart from the obvious flat battery, is the battery earth lead connection not making proper contact with the body or chassis of the vehicle.
If this is the problem, remove the connector and clean as with the main battery terminals.
Check both battery cables and any earth straps for breakage or fraying (this usually occurs at the terminal ends) and replace them if necessary.
Finally, check the level of the battery electrolyte – that is the fluid inside the battery – which should be just above the battery plates.
If the battery plates are exposed, top them up using distilled water. Some batteries are sealed for life and topping up is not possible.
Remember radio and alarm codes may be lost.

Safety tips

Never smoke whilst working in the vicinity of the battery as it could be giving off an explosive gas.
When disconnecting or reconnecting the live battery terminal, be very careful not to allow the spanner to contact any metalwork of the car. This could give you a bad burn or the resulting spark could cause a battery to explode.
To be on the safe side, always remove the battery earth cable first – that is the one connected to the bodywork, chassis or engine – and reconnect it last.

Ignition system

Before attempting to carry out any checks or adjustments on any part of the ignition system, you must ensure that the ignition is switched off.

Contact points*
Remove the distributor cap and this will expose the contact points. The contact points are the most common cause of breakdown in the ignition system. If the contact point faces appear badly pitted or burnt then they will require replacing or cleaning.
The contact point gap is also critical, this can close up after a period of time. Contact point gaps vary from one model to another so consult your vehicle handbook.
To check and adjust the contact point gap, it is necessary to rotate the engine until one of the lobes on the distributor cam has pushed the moving arm of the contact points to its fullest open position.
Using a feeler gauge, make any adjustment to the gap by slackening the contact breaker retaining screw or screws and move the position of the contact points relative to the distributor base plate.
This can usually be best achieved by placing a screwdriver between the adjustment notches and turning.
Adjust the contact point gap until the feeler gauge will just fit between the contact points.
Lock the adjusting screw and re-check the gap as sometimes the setting can alter when the retaining screw is tightened.
*Not electronic ignition systems

Distributor cap
The distributor cap is another potential problem area. Carry out the following simple checks:
1 Check the H.T. leads are secure in the cap.
2 Make sure the distributor cap is free from any oil residue, dirt or moisture both inside and outside.
3 Examine the rotor arm and distributor cap very closely both inside and outside for any hairline cracks or tracking caused by the H.T. current.
4 Whilst the distributor cap is removed, check the centre connector. This should protrude far enough to contact the rotor arm when the cap is replaced. If the carbon brush is badly worn then a replacement cap will be needed.

H.T. leads
The H.T. leads are the thick cables coming out of the distributor cap. Any breakdown either in the conductive centre, the insulation or at the connections will cause faulty operation of the ignition system.
First, wipe the outer insulation material clean and examine for cracking or deterioration.
Check the connectors at both ends for security and cleanliness.
The H.T. leads to the spark plugs must be fitted in the correct positions; if the leads are mixed up, the car will not start.
It is a good idea to number the leads to assist you in correct re-installation. Alternatively, only remove one H.T. lead at a time.
Modern vehicles are fitted with carbon core type leads which can break down internally. This type of lead can be properly tested only by an auto electrician.

Coil connections
The coil is the source of power for the ignition system and it is vital that the connections for the two low-tension wires either side of the main H.T. lead are both secure and clean.
Check the main H.T. lead to ensure this is secure.
Examine the plastic top of the coil for hairline cracks or tracking caused by the H.T. current short-circuiting and replace if need be.
Finally ensure the coil top is clean of grease, dirt or damp.

Fuel system

It is far more difficult to anticipate a breakdown in the fuel system although some simple checks can be carried out to minimise the risk.

1 Examine any rubber fuel pipes for age cracking, softening, leakage, and make sure they are secure at the connections.

2 Most vehicle fuel systems will incorporate a fuel filter or dirt trap to prevent any debris being transmitted through the fuel lines to the carburettor. Ensure that the periodic checks detailed in the vehicle handbook are carried out – usually either cleaning or replacement.

3 Check around the carburettor gasket joints, jet assemblies, and feed pipes for any evidence of fuel leakage. Rectification may require the services of a specialist.

4 The efficiency of the engine will greatly depend upon the correct mixture setting for the carburettor. With modern carburettors, this can be checked and reset only by a properly equipped workshop. Excessive exhaust emissions now constitute a legal offence.

Cooling system

The efficiency of the engine cooling system is vital when contemplating a continental touring holiday, as the climatic conditions and terrain may impose greater strains upon the system.

Check the radiator to ensure it is free from external blockage or restrictions. Remove any debris such as leaves, paper or dirt.

Inspect all the rubber coolant hoses for signs of age cracking, bulges (particularly adjacent to the securing clips) and check tightness of hose clips, although avoid overtightening as this will cut into the hose material.

When topping up the cooling system, it is advisable to do so with the recommended anti-freeze solution, as anti-freeze contains a corrosion inhibitor to minimise the corrosion build-up.

Check the fan belt for fraying, general deterioration or excessive glazing on the V-shape drive surfaces, as these may promote slip If there is more than half an inch of free play on the belt's longest run, some adjustment is required.

If the fan belt has not been replaced during the preceding 12 months, then it is a good idea to replace it to avoid any possible inconvenience should it fail. Keep the old fan belt in the boot as a 'get you home' spare.

If your fan belt does break, then this will be signalled by the generator/ignition warning light lighting up and an increased reading on the water temperature gauge if one is fitted.

The car should be stopped immediately and the belt replaced, in order to minimise any damage that might be caused to the engine.

On many diesel engines the brake servo pump is driven by the alternator drive belt and the brakes will, therefore, lose efficiency.

Finally, do not forget other parts of the vehicle that can break down and cause you considerable inconvenience.

Tyres should be checked for condition, tread depth and pressure.

Check the exhaust system for condition and security.

Last, but certainly not least, check the braking system. If you do not feel competent to do so, call in the experts.

Tyres

Tyre pressure

Tyre pressures should be checked weekly, using a reliable gauge, and corrected as necessary. Pressure tests and correction of pressure should be made with the tyres cold and not after a period of running.

It may be necessary to increase pressures because of loading or high speeds, particularly in hot countries (refer to the vehicle handbook). Both car and tyre manufacturers provide details of correct pressures for various types of driving conditions. Under-inflation is a frequent cause of tyre failure.

Tread depth of tyres

By law, you must maintain a tread pattern of at least 1.6mm in one continuous band across three-quarters of the tread and around the entire circumference of each tyre.

It is advisable to ensure that your spare tyre also complies with this regulation.

Wheel alignment

Wheel alignment should be checked when abnormal front tyre wear is noted, and after even a minor front-end collision.

Shock absorbers

Worn shock absorbers can affect the stability of a car and the life of the tyres.

Shock absorbers should be checked visually for oil leaks, and by bouncing the appropriate corner of the car, and replaced when necessary.

Wheel balance

Wheels should be balanced whenever a tyre is changed or when vibration or wobble becomes apparent.

Tyre damage

Tyres can be damaged easily by nails, sharp stones, kerbs etc. Avoid brushing against kerbs – this can damage the sidewalls.

If you have to drive up a kerb, do so slowly and at as near a right angle as possible to minimise any damage. Inspect tyres regularly; remove any stones or nails lodged in the tread.

It is illegal to drive on a tyre which has a break in its fabric, or a cut over 1 inch long and deep enough to reach the body cords.

Tyre life

Maximum tyre life is largely in the driver's hands, although chassis design and maintenance also play a part. Prolonging tyre life usually means that the performance of the car cannot be exploited to its full extent; thus the driver can choose between obtaining maximum performance from the car or maximum life from the tyres.

Tyre life can be prolonged by:
- taking corners easily;
- avoiding high average speeds, especially on rough surfaces;
- avoiding rapid acceleration and/or violent braking;
- keeping brakes properly adjusted;
- avoiding damage by oil, grease, petrol, paraffin, etc;
- maintaining correct pressures.

Ferry Routes

Belgium

Dover–Ostend 2 hr 5 mins *Hoverspeed SeaCat* – up to 7 per day

Hull–Zeebrugge 14 hr *P&O North Sea Ferries* – 1 per day

Denmark

Harwich–Esbjerg 19 hr 30 mins–20 hr *Scandinavian Seaways* – up to 3 per week

France

Dover–Calais 1 hr 30 mins *P&O Stena Line* (catamaran/ferry) – up to 24 per day; 1 hr 30 mins Sea France (ferry) – 15 per day; 35–50 mins *Hoverspeed Hovercraft/SeaCat* – up to 14 per day

Folkestone–Boulogne 55 mins *Hoverspeed Seacat* – up to 6 per day

Newhaven–Dieppe 2 hr *Hoverspeed* (fast ferry) April-September – 3 per day

Plymouth–Roscoff 6 hr *Brittany Ferries* – up to 3 per day (summer), up to 3 per week (winter)

Poole–Cherbourg 4 hr 15 mins *Brittany Ferries* – 2 per day

Portsmouth–Caen 6 hr *Brittany Ferries* – up to 3 per day

Portsmouth–Cherbourg (ferry) (day) 5 hr, (night) 7–8 hr 15 mins (catamaran) 2 hr 45 mins *P&O European Ferries* – up to 4 per day

Portsmouth–Le Havre (day) 5 hr 30 mins (night) 7 hr 30 mins–8 hr *P&O European Ferries* – up to 3 per day

Portsmouth–St Malo 9 hr *Brittany Ferries* – 1 per day (up to 2 per week in winter)

Services from Ireland to France

Cork–Roscoff 4 hr *Brittany Ferries* – 2 per week

Rosslare–Cherbourg 17 hr 30 mins *Irish Ferries* (contact operator for details)

Rosslare–Roscoff 16 hr *Irish Ferries* (contact operator for details)

Germany

Harwich–Hamburg 23 hr *Scandinavian Seaways* – 3–4 per week

Newcastle-upon-Tyne–Hamburg 23 hr 30 mins *Scandinavian Seaways* – every 4 days (summer)

Ireland

Northern Ireland

Cairnryan–Larne 1 hr (jetferry) 2 hrs 15 mins (ferry) *P&O European Ferries* – up to 9 per day

Stranraer–Belfast (catamaran) 1 hr 45 mins *Stena Line* – up to 9 per day

Stranraer–Belfast 1 hr 30 mins *SeaCat Scotland* – up to 4 per day

Liverpool–Belfast 9 hr 30 mins *Norse Irish Ferries* – 10 per week

Republic of Ireland

Fishguard–Rosslare (ferry) 3 hr 30 mins *Stena Line* – up to 2 per day; (catamaran) 1hr 39 mins Stena Line – 4 per day

Holyhead–Dublin 3 hr 15 mins *Irish Ferries* – 2 per day. Fast ferry from June 1999 1 hr 50 mins

Liverpool–Dublin 3 hr 50 mins *Isle of Man Steam Packet Co* – up to 2 daily

Holyhead–Dun Laoghaire (ferry) 3 hr 45 mins
Stena Line – up to 2 per day; (catamaran)
1 hr 40 mins *Stena Line* – up to 5 per day

Pembroke Dock–Rosslare 4 hr *Irish Ferries*
– up to 2 per day

Swansea–Cork 10 hr *Swansea Cork
Ferries* – 6 per week

Netherlands

Harwich–Hoek van Holland (catamaran)
3 hr 40 mins *Stena Line* – 2 per day

Hull–Rotterdam (Europoort) 12 hr 30 mins
P&O North Sea Ferries – 1 per day

Newcastle–Amsterdam 15–17 hr 30 mins
Scandinavian Seaways – 3 per week

Norway

Newcastle upon Tyne–Bergen 19–25 hr
30 mins *Fjord Line* – 3 per week (summer)
2 per week (winter)

Newcastle upon Tyne–Stavanger 17–27 hr
30 mins *Fjord Line* – 3 per week (summer)
2 per week (winter)

Newcastle upon Tyne–Haugesund 19–25 hr
45 mins *Fjord Line* – 2 per week

Spain

Plymouth–Santander (from mid March)
23–24 hr *Brittany Ferries* – up to 2 per
week

Portsmouth/Poole–Santander (winter only)
30–31 hr *Brittany Ferries* – 1 per week

Portsmouth–Bilbao 30–35 hr *P&O
European Ferries* – 2 per week

Sweden

Harwich–Göteborg 23 hr *Scandinavian
Seaways* – up to 2 per week

Newcastle-upon-Tyne–Göteborg via
Kristiansand, Norway 23–24 hr
Scandinavian Seaways – 2 per week

Ferry companies

P&O European Ferries

Channel House, Channel View Road, Dover
CT17 9TJ   Reservations: 0990 980 980
Calais   Tel: 03 21 46 04 40
Cairnryan   Tel: 0990 980 666
Le Havre   Tel: 02 35 19 78 50
Cherbourg   Tel: 02 33 88 65 70
Portsmouth   Tel: 0990 980 555
Larne   Tel: 0990 980 777
Bilbao   Tel: (94) 423 4477

Sea France

106 East Camber Bdg, East Docks, Dover
CT16 1JA   Reservations: 0990 711 711

Stena Line

Charter House, Ashford, Kent, TN24 8EX
           Reservations: 0990 707 070
Calais   Tel: 03 21 46 80 00
Cherbourg   Tel: 02 33 20 43 38
Dieppe   Tel: 02 35 06 39 00
Hoek van Holland   Tel: 47 82 351

Hoverspeed Ltd

International Hoverport, Western Dock, Dover,
Kent CT17 9TG
Reservations: 0870 524 0241 – French Routes
              0870 559 5522 – Ostend Route
Boulogne   Tel: 03 21 30 27 26
Calais   Tel: 03 21 46 14 14

Scandinavian Seaways

Scandinavia House, Parkeston Quay, Harwich,
Essex CO12 4QG   Reservations: 0990 333 111
Esbjerg   Tel: 75 12 48 00
Göteborg   Tel: (031) 65 06 00
Hamburg   Tel: (040) 3 89 03 71

Brittany Ferries

Millbay Docks, Plymouth PL1 3EW:
The Brittany Centre, Wharf Road, Portsmouth PO2
8RU   Reservations: 0990 360 360
Caen   Tel: 02 31 96 88 80
Cherbourg   Tel: 02 33 43 43 68
Cork   Tel: (021) 277801
Roscoff   Tel: 02 98 29 28 28
Santander   Tel: 22 00 00
St Malo   Tel: 02 99 40 64 41

Fjord Line

International Ferry Terminal, Royal Quays,
North Shields NE29 6EG
           Reservations: 0191-296 1313

P&O North Sea Ferries

King George Dock, Hedon Road, Hull
HU9 5QA   Reservations: (01482) 377177

Irish Ferries

2–4 Merrion Row, Dublin 2, Irish Republic
           Reservations: 0990 17 17 17

Isle of Man Steam Packet Co

PO Box 5, Douglas, Isle of Man IM99 1AF
                      Tel: 01624 661661

Norse Irish Ferries

Victoria Terminal 2, West Bank Road, Belfast
BT3 9JN   Tel: 01232 779090

Swansea Cork Ferries

The Ferry Port, Swansea SA1 8RU
           Reservations: (01792) 456116

Channel Tunnel
Eurotunnel

Cheriton Parc, Cheriton High Street, Folkestone
CT19 4QS   Reservations: 0990 35 35 35

Time differences

In many European countries, local time is altered during the summer, in the same way it is in the UK.
Although most European countries are one hour ahead of the UK throughout the year, there is a period in October when European Summer Time has ended but when British Summer Time has not.
Note:
The Baltic States, Bulgaria, Finland, Greece, Romania and Turkey are two hours ahead of Greenwich Mean Time.
In Portugal, the time is the same as in Great Britain.

Introduction

In this section of the Guide, essential motoring information and valuable general information is given in detail for each individual country. Driving in Europe can present the motorist with many unfamiliar problems, and advice on several of those likely to be encountered is presented here by way of an introduction.

'Bison Fute'

In France you will see signs for exits off the autoroutes marked *Bis* on an orange panel. This is short for *Bison Futé*, and indicates alternative routes which avoid areas prone to congestion at peak periods.

A free map of 'Bis' routes is published in June each year by the French Government; contact RAC Travel Information (Tel: 0891 347 333) or Maison de la France (Tel: 0891 244 123). Calls cost 60p per minute at all times.

Drinking and driving

Many motorists believe that they are safe with a blood alcohol level of 50 or 80mg: they are wrong. Even at a level of 20mg, signs of impaired concentration may register. Remember that factors like fatigue, illness or stress have additional effects, and may cause severe concentration loss even when only small amounts of alcohol are consumed. Blood alcohol limits are given for each country.

Penalties for exceeding these limits can be very severe. The limit in the UK is 80mg.

Fuel

Information on the availability and octane rating of leaded and unleaded petrol, translations for unleaded petrol, and regulations concerning the carriage of spare fuel are detailed for each country.

The grades are shown as:
- 'Regular' (the cheapest)
- 'Super' (covering both 'Premium' and 'Super' grades in Europe, which correspond to the two British grades).

The best guide to the grade is price. If you use 'Super' in the UK, then use the most expensive abroad.

Where three grades are available, do not use the lowest unless you are sure that your car will run on it.

Where only one grade is available, this is likely to be the equivalent of the cheaper UK grade.

The current prices of petrol and diesel in the European countries are available from RAC Travel Information (Tel: 0891 347 333).

If in doubt, contact the car manufacturer prior to departure.

If paying by credit card, visitors are strongly advised to check that the amount of fuel purchased tallies with the figure on the voucher before signing.

Level crossings

A level crossing is indicated by three roadside signals, set at 80m intervals before the point where the road and railway cross.

At the level crossing, approaching trains are often indicated by a beacon flashing red intermittently; this changes to white or amber when there are no trains approaching.

Some level crossings do not have gates or barriers, and an approaching train is indicated by a flashing red light or continuous bell.

Headlights must not be on when waiting at a level crossing after dark.

Mountain roads

Strong winds can affect steering, and a firm grip on the wheel is necessary. Even in summer, mist is not uncommon at high altitudes. If you are unsure of your position on a mountain, draw well into your own side of the road, stop the car (keeping the lights on), and wait until visibility improves.
Traffic descending should give way to that ascending. Postal vans and coaches (usually marked with a bugle sign) have priority, and any instructions given by their drivers must be followed.

Overheating

In hot weather generally, the level of water in the radiator needs to be checked frequently.
If the radiator has lost water but the level is still above the bottom of the header tank, water may be added immediately, provided the engine is allowed to tick over and mix the cold water with the hot water in the engine.
If the system has run dry, the engine must be allowed to cool before water is added, otherwise the cylinder block may be severely damaged.
If you suspect that the water in the radiator is overheating, do not attempt to open the radiator cap immediately. Allow the water to cool first.
High temperatures and prolonged ascents can cause petrol to vaporise in the fuel lines, pump or carburettor, and the engine will stop.
If this happens, allow the engine to cool; a damp cloth placed over the engine will speed the cooling process.

Overloading

Each passenger should have a fixed seat, and the luggage weight should not exceed that recommended by the manufacturer's handbook. Take care not to overload the roof rack; Switzerland, for example, normally applies a 50kg limit to roof rack loads.
In the case of an accident, the driver of an overloaded vehicle could be prosecuted and might find himself inadequately covered by insurance.
The French authorities in particular, are concerned by the serious overloading of many British-registered cars touring France.

Overtaking

In Europe, one of the main problems for drivers of right-hand drive vehicles is overtaking, as vehicles in front block the view of the road ahead.
It is necessary to keep well back from the vehicle in front in order to see whether it is safe to overtake.
A mirror fitted on the left-hand side of the car will prove useful.

Roundabouts

These are often confusing for British drivers.
In Germany, Sweden, Denmark and Norway, if there is a 'Give Way' sign, traffic on a roundabout has priority, as in the UK.
In France, it is now normal for traffic on a roundabout to have priority: a triangular sign with a red border showing a roundabout symbol with the legend *vous n'avez pas la priorité* indicates this.
However, in a few areas the old ruling of priority given to traffic entering a roundabout still applies. So, where the above sign is not present, you should approach with care.
In all other countries, traffic on a roundabout should give way to traffic wishing to enter.

Safety

There have been a growing number of reports concerning a modern form of 'highway robbery' on some trunk routes through France and Spain. Although such incidents are minimal in relation to the thousands of journeys made to those countries, it could be well worth bearing in mind that the seemingly friendly stranger – only too keen to hear about your planned route and destination – may be making some plans of his own.
Many countries in Europe have undergone change recently, both peaceful and violent. Contact the FCO for advice.
Travel advice may be obtained from the Foreign and Commonwealth Office Travel Advice Unit (Tel: 0171-238 4503/4504).

Notes to chart on pages 17–20

1   A new photocard UK licence is being introduced which is believed will be accepted almost everywhere in Europe.
EC model format UK licences (pink or pink/green) accepted. Austria: old style green licences only accepted if accompanied by an identity document with photograph, e.g. passport. Lithuania: UK licence accepted if accompanied by identity document bearing a photograph e.g. passport. Hungary, Italy, Poland, Portugal, Romania, Spain: holder of old style green licences require an International Driving Permit, available from RAC.
Green style licences can be exchanged by completing DVLA form D1 from any post office.

2   Minimum age at which a visiting motorist can drive a temporarily imported vehicle.

3   Camping Card International not recognised by Svenska Campingvärdars Riksförbund (SCR) campsites.

4   Motorists should carry evidence of motor insurance (insurance certificate). A Green Card provides additional proof that the minimum legal third party cover is held. For further advice please contact your insurance company.
A Green Card is compulsory in Andorra and strongly recommended in Greece, Hungary, Italy, Portugal and Spain.
Your Green Card should be valid for both the European and Asian sections when visiting Turkey.
In Bulgaria, Poland and Romania visiting motorists must take out short term insurance at the border on arrival. Lithuania is not part of the Green Card system and short term insurance must be arranged at the border. Cover for the CIS may be taken out through the insurance agency (Ingosstrakh) – there are offices in various European countries. It is also available on arrival at the frontier at Brest (Polish border) and Uzhgorod (Slovakia/Ukraine border).

5   Warning triangle or hazard warning lights are acceptable, but motorists are strongly recommended to carry a warning triangle in their vehicle.

6   Two warning triangles are compulsory for vehicles with 9 seats or more.

7   A motorway tax disc must be displayed on all vehicles using certain motorways in Austria. Weekly/monthly/annual discs are available at major border crossings, petrol stations and post offices.

8   A toll is charged to enter Oslo, Bergen and Trondheim.

9   A motorway tax disc must be displayed by all vehicles using Swiss motorways. A disc valid for 1 year can be obtained from Switzerland Tourism in London or at border crossings. A motorway toll sticker valid for 1 year must be displayed in the front windscreen of vehicles using motorways in the Czech Republic and certain motorways in Slovakia.

10 Leaded regular petrol no longer available in Belgium, Denmark, France, Luxembourg, Norway, Switzerland. Super leaded petrol available.

11 Leaded petrol no longer available in Austria, Finland, Germany, Netherlands, Sweden. Certain pumps dispensing unleaded petrol contain a lead additive, for vehicles requiring leaded petrol.

12 International Driving Permit also required in Bulgaria, CIS, and Czech Republic. However, it is believed the new style photocard full UK licence will be accepted in Bulgaria, Czech Republic and Hungary.

13 In Turkey a UK driving licence is recognised for 3 months only.

Documents/Legal	ANDORRA	AUSTRIA	BELGIUM	BULGARIA	CIS	CROATIA	CYPRUS (SOUTH)	CZECH REPUBLIC	DENMARK
UK Driving Lic. (full)	YES	YES	YES	YES (12)	YES (12)	YES	YES	YES (12)	YES
Drivers (minimum age)	18	18	18	18	18	18	18	18	18
Camping Card Int.	R	R	R	R	R	R	R	R	R
Green Card/Motor Ins.	C (4)	R	R	R (4)	Not Valid (4)	R	R	R	R
GB Sticker	C	C	C	C	C	C	C	C	C
Crash Helmets	C	C	C	C	C	C	R	C	C
Seat Belts (rear if fitted)	C	C	C	C	C	C	C	C	C

Motoring Accessories	ANDORRA	AUSTRIA	BELGIUM	BULGARIA	CIS	CROATIA	CYPRUS (SOUTH)	CZECH REPUBLIC	DENMARK
Spare Bulbs	R	R	R	R	R	C	R	R	R
Warning Triangle	C	C	C	C	C	C	C	C	C
First Aid Kit	R	C	R	R	C	C	R	C	R
Fire Extinguisher	R	R	R	C	C	R	R	C	R
Headlamp converter	YES	YES	YES	YES	YES	YES	NO	YES	YES

General	ANDORRA	AUSTRIA	BELGIUM	BULGARIA	CIS	CROATIA	CYPRUS (SOUTH)	CZECH REPUBLIC	DENMARK
Motorway Tolls (private cars)	NO	YES (7)	NO	YES	NO	YES	NO	YES (9)	NO
Petrol	YES	YES (11)	YES (10)	YES	YES (Leaded)	YES	YES	YES	YES (10)
Availability of leaded/unleaded					NO (Unleaded)				

Key
R – Recommended
C – Compulsory

Documents/Legal	ESTONIA	FINLAND	FRANCE	GERMANY	GIBRALTAR	GREECE	HUNGARY	IRELAND	ITALY
UK Driving Lic. (full)	YES	YES	YES	YES	YES	YES	YES (1)	YES	YES
Drivers (minimum age)	18	18	18	17	18	18	18	17	18
Camping Card Int.	R	R	R	R	R	R	R	Not Req	R
Green Card/Motor Ins.	R	R	R	R	R	R	R (4)	R	R
GB Sticker	C	C	C	C	C	C	C	C	C
Crash Helmets	R	C	C	C	C	C	C	C	C
Seat Belts (rear if fitted)	R	C	C	C	R	R	C	C	C

Motoring Accessories	ESTONIA	FINLAND	FRANCE	GERMANY	GIBRALTAR	GREECE	HUNGARY	IRELAND	ITALY
Spare Bulbs	R	R	R	R	R	R	R	R	R
Warning Triangle	R	C	R (5)	C	R	C	C	R	C
First Aid Kit	C	R	R	R	R	C	R	R	R
Fire Extinguisher	C	R	R	R	R	C	R	R	R
Headlamp converter	YES	YES	YES	YES	YES	YES	YES	NO	YES

General	ESTONIA	FINLAND	FRANCE	GERMANY	GIBRALTAR	GREECE	HUNGARY	IRELAND	ITALY
Motorway Tolls (private cars)	NO	NO	YES	NO	NO	YES	YES	NO	YES
Petrol	YES	YES (11)	YES (10)	YES (11)	YES	YES	YES	YES	YES
Availability of leaded/unleaded									

Key
R – Recommended
C – Compulsory

	LATVIA	LITHUANIA	LUXEMBOURG	NETHERLANDS	NORWAY	POLAND	PORTUGAL	ROMANIA	SLOVAKIA
Documents/Legal									
UK Driving Lic. (full)	YES	YES (1)	YES	YES	YES	YES (1)	YES	YES (1)	YES
Drivers (minimum age)	18	18	18	18	17	18	17	18	18
Camping Card Int.	R	R	R	R	R	R	R	R	R
Green Card/Motor Ins.	R	Not Valid (4)	R	R	R	R (4)	R	R (4)	R
GB Sticker	C	C	C	C	C	C	C	C	C
Crash Helmets	R	R	C	C	C	C	C	C	R
Seat Belts (rear if fitted)	R	R	C	R	C	C	C	R	C
Motoring Accessories									
Spare Bulbs	R	R	R	R	R	R	R	R	R
Warning Triangle	C	C	C	C	C (5)	C	C	C	C
First Aid Kit	C	C	R	R	R	R	R	C	C
Fire Extinguisher	C	C	R	R	R	R	R	R	R
Headlamp converter	YES	YES	YES	YES	YES	YES	YES	YES	YES
General									
Motorway Tolls (private cars)	NO	NO	NO	NO	YES (8)	NO	YES	NO	YES (9)
Petrol	YES	YES	YES (11)	YES (11)	YES (11)	YES	YES	YES	YES
Availability of leaded/unleaded									

Key
R – Recommended
C – Compulsory

	SLOVENIA	SPAIN	SWEDEN	SWITZERLAND	TURKEY	UNITED KINGDOM
Documents/Legal						
UK Driving Lic. (full)	YES	YES (1)	YES	YES	YES (13)	YES
Drivers (minimum age)	18	18	18	18	17	17
Camping Card Int.	R	R	R(3)	R	R	Not req.
Green Card/Motor Ins.	R	R	R	R	R (4)	N/A
GB Sticker	C	C	C	C	C	NO
Crash Helmets	R	C	C	C	C	C
Seat Belts (rear if fitted)	C	C	C	C	C	C
Motoring Accessories						
Spare Bulbs	R	C	R	R	R	R
Warning Triangle	C	R (6)	R	C	C	R
First Aid Kit	C	R	R	R	C	R
Fire Extinguisher	R	R	R	R	C	R
Headlamp converter	YES	YES	YES	YES	Y ES	NO
General						
Motorway Tolls (private cars)	YES	YES	NO	YES (9)	YES	NO
Petrol	YES	YES	YES (11)	YES (10)	YES	YES
Availability of leaded/unleaded						

Key
R – Recommended
C – Compulsory

Albania

At the time of going to print travel is not recommended in Albania.

Embassy

Embassy of the Republic of Albania,
4th floor, 38 Grosvenor Gardens, London
SW1W 0EB. Tel: 0171-730 5709.

Andorra

National motoring organisation

Automobil Club d'Andorra, FIA, Babot Camp 4, Andorra la Vieja. Tel: 20-8-90.

Accidents and emergencies

Police Tel: 17; Fire Brigade, Ambulance Tel: 18.

Fuel

Leaded petrol: Super (98 octane) available.

Speed limits

Built-up areas: 25mph (40kmh); outside built-up areas: 44mph (70kmh). The police are empowered to collect on-the-spot fines.

Banks

Open Mon–Fri 0900–1300 and 1500–1700, Sat 0900–1300.

Currency

French francs and Spanish pesetas.

Public holidays

Canillo, third Sat in July; St Julia de Loria, last Sun in July and following Mon and Tue; Escaldos Engerdany, 25, 26 and 27 July; Andorra la Vieja, first Sat in Aug, and following Sun and Mon; La Massana, 15, 16 and 17 Aug; Meritxett Pilgrimage, 8 Sep; Ordino, 16, 17 Sep.

Shops

Open daily 0900–2000 (except 8 Sep).

Tourist office

Andorran Delegation, 63 Westover Road, London SW18 2RF, Tel: 0181-874 4806

Austria

National motoring organisation

Österreichischer Automobil, Motorrad-und Touring Club (ÖAMTC), FIA, Schubertring 1–3, 1010 Wien (Vienna) 1. Tel: 1-711 990. Office hours: weekdays 0800–1700. Closed Sat/Sun and public holidays, except the breakdown assistance service.

Accidents and emergencies

Police Tel: 133, Fire Brigade Tel: 122, Ambulance Tel: 144. Alternatively 112 for all services.

Breakdowns

The ÖAMTC operate a Breakdown and Technical Assistance service on major roads throughout Austria, Tel: 120 (24-hr Breakdown service, Wien).

Caravans

Drivers of motorcaravans and towed caravans are strongly recommended not to overload such vehicles. The caravan weight should not exceed that of the towing vehicle. Checks are undertaken at border crossings to ensure this regulation is not infringed.

Carriage of children

Children under 12 and less than 1.5 metres in height are not permitted to travel on the front or rear seat, unless a special seat or seat belt is used. Children under 12 but over 1.5 metres in height must use the adult seat belt.

Drinking and driving

The blood alcohol legal limit is 50mg.

Driving licence

UK licences bearing a photograph of the holder accepted otherwise it must be accompanied by an identity document with photograph, e.g. passport. EC licences (pink/pink and green) are accepted.

Fuel

Most petrol stations are open 0800-2000, and many operate 24 hours a day in large cities.
Leaded petrol: Super has been withdrawn from sale. Super Plus (98 octane), containing a special lead additive, should be used by vehicles unable to take unleaded petrol.
Unleaded petrol: Regular (91 octane) and Super (98 octane) available; pump legend *bleifrei normal* or *bleifrei super.*
Diesel: available.
Credit cards: rarely accepted as payment for fuel, apart from the AVANTI chain who accept charge and credit cards.
Spare fuel: 10 litres of petrol in a can may be imported duty free in addition to the fuel in the tank.

Hitchhiking

Prohibited on motorways and dual carriageways. In Styria, Upper Austria, Burgenland and the Vorarlberg hitchhiking is prohibited for people under 16.

Lighting

Dipped headlights are compulsory in built-up areas. No parking lights are required if the vehicle can be seen from a distance of about 55 yards (50 metres).
If visibility is bad, sidelights should be on. Mopeds and motorcycles must use lights at all times.

Orange Badge holders

Orange badge holders may park without time limit where a round blue and red no waiting sign is used. Where a round blue and red no stopping sign is displayed (waiting/parking prohibited for longer than 10 minutes) they may stop for loading/unloading beyond the time limit.
Badge holders may also park in a pedestrian zone

where loading/unloading is allowed, but only during the times indicated. Parking is also allowed without time limit in areas normally reserved for short term parking.
Special parking places for disabled people's vehicles may also be provided near hospitals and public service facilities for the care of people with disabilities.

Overtaking

Overtake vehicles on the left. Overtaking on the right is permitted only when overtaking trams, in one-way streets, or when overtaking vehicles indicating left. Do not cross or straddle the continuous yellow line at the centre of the road. Motorists should not overtake a parked school bus with flashing red and yellow lights.

Parking

Do not park in the following areas (except for a short wait of 10 minutes):
(a) At places indicated by 'No parking' signs.
(b) Where there are crosses on the roadway, in front of houses, entrances, or petrol stations.
(c) On narrow roads, on the left in one-way streets, or on priority roads outside built-up areas at dusk, in darkness, fog or any road condition which reduces visibility.
Do not park or wait where a sign says *Halten Verboten* (no waiting). In Baden, Bludenz, Bregenz, Feldkirch, Graz, Innsbruck, Klagenfurt, Krems, Linz, St Pölten, Salzburg, Schwaz, Wien, Villach and Wiener Neustadt, a fee is charged for motor vehicles parked in the Blue Zone.
Motorists must buy parking tickets in advance from banks, tobacconists etc.
The date and time of arrival must be indicated on the ticket and displayed on the windscreen. Unless otherwise indicated under the *Kurzparkzone* (short-term parking) road sign, parking is allowed for up to three hours.
In other towns parking is free for up to 90 mins in Blue Zones. Parking tickets are not required but a parking disc must be used for all vehicles including motorcycles.
This disc can be obtained free of charge from tobacconists. Illegally parked cars may be towed away.
Do not leave a caravan trailer without its towing vehicle in a public parking place (e.g. motorway service area).
In the Tyrol, Upper Austria and Salzburg, it is

prohibited to park caravans outside specially authorised parking places or within 500 metres of a lake. Do not park caravans within 200 metres of the Grossglockner High Alpine Road and the motorway in Salzburg. Heavy fines and forcible removal of a caravan can result if these regulations are not observed.

Pedestrian crossings

In most large towns where there are traffic light controlled junctions without pedestrian lights, pedestrians may cross only when the lights are green for travelling in the same direction. Do not wait at the edge of the kerb.

Priority

Priority is given to main roads or those roads bearing the 'Main Road' symbol.
On roads of equal importance, priority is given to traffic approaching from the right.
Do give priority to trams coming from the left, also to police cars and all emergency vehicles with a flashing blue light and multi-toned sirens.
When passing traffic on mountain roads, ascending vehicles have priority.

Road signs

Most conform to the international pattern. Other road conditions may be indicated as follows:
Anhänger Verboten: trailers not allowed
Ausweiche: detour
Beschränkung für Halten oder Parken: stopping or parking restricted
Halten Verboten: no waiting
Hupverbot: use of horn prohibited
Lawinen Gefahr: avalanche danger
Querstrasse: crossroads
Steinschlag: falling rocks
Strasse Gesperrt: road closed

Signalling

Give warning of approach by flashing headlamps. Horns may not be used where their use is prohibited by a road sign. This applies in many large towns, mostly at night, and in Wien at all times.

Speed limits

Built-up areas: 31mph (50kmh); outside built-up areas: 62mph (100kmh); motorways: 81mph (130kmh).

Speed limits are lowered to 68mph (110kmh) between 2200 and 0500 on the following motorways: A8 (Innkreis), A9 (Pyhrn), A10 (Tauern), A12 (Inntal), A13 (Brenner), A14 (Rheintal).
Minimum speed limit on motorways and roads displaying a rectangular blue sign bearing a white car is 60kmh.
Cars towing a caravan or a trailer under 750kg are restricted to 62mph (100kmh) on all roads outside built-up areas, this includes on motorways.
If the trailer is over 750kg contact RAC Travel Information Tel: 0891 347 333 (call charged at 60p per minute) for guidance on speed limits.

Tolls

As of 1 January 1997, a tax disc must be displayed on all vehicles using Austrian motorways. For information, see page 74.

Traffic offences

Police are empowered to impose and collect on-the-spot fines up to AS 500.
The police officer collecting the fine must issue an official receipt.
The motorist may pay the fine during the following two weeks, and with the original paying-in slip; the fine is payable in most European currencies.
Motorists refusing to pay, may request that the case be brought before a police court; however, the police may ask for a security to be deposited.

General information

Banks

Open Mon–Fri 0800–1230 and 1330–1500 (Thu 1330–1730).

Currency

Austrian Schilling.

Public holidays

New Year's Day; Epiphany; Easter Monday; Labour Day; Ascension; Whit Monday; Corpus Christi; Assumption, 15 Aug; National Day, 26 Oct; All Saints, 1 Nov; Immaculate Conception, 8 Dec; Christmas, 25, 26 Dec.

Shops

Open Mon–Fri 0800–1930, with a one or two hour break at midday. Sat 0800–1300. In central Wien shops do not close for lunch.

Tourist office

Austrian National Tourist Office, 30 St George Street, London W1R 0AL, Tel: 0171-629 0461 Official website: www.austria-tourism.at

Baltic States

Motoring information

National motoring organisations

Latvia: Auto-Moto Society of Latvia (LR AMB), FIA, 16B Raunas, LV-1039 Riga. Tel: (371) 2 56 83 39, 56 62 22
Lithuania: Association of Lithuanian Automobilists LAS, FIA, Lvovo 9, 2005 Vilnius. Tel: (370) 2 35 12 73, 35 21 86.

Accidents and emergencies

Police Tel: 02, Fire Brigade Tel: 01, Ambulance Tel: 03 or 112. When an accident occurs, you must contact the police.

Breakdowns

The Finnish oil company, Neste Oy, provides a 24-hr roadside breakdown assistance service, along the 'Via Baltica'. The emergency numbers are: (370) 2 53 43 86 or 53 42 91.

Drinking and driving

Do not drink and drive: blood alcohol legal limit is 0mg.

Ferries

Car ferry services operate on the following routes:

Estonia:	Operator
Helsinki (Finland) – Tallinn.	*Tallink Silja*
Stockholm (Sweden) – Tallinn.	*Estline*
Latvia:	
Rostock (Germany) – Liepaja.	*Euroseabridge*
Lithuania:	
Kiel (Germany) – Klaipeda.	*Lita Shipping*
Mukran (Germany) – Klaipeda	*Euroseabridge*

Fuel

Availability of fuel has improved with the establishment of a chain of 11 service stations by Neste Oy along the M-12 ('Via Baltica') motorway. These are located every 150km (90 miles) and are open 24 hours. Service stations may be found in Tallinn (2), Parnu, Savikrasti (north of Riga), Riga (2), Kekava, Panevezys, Marijampole and Vilnius (2).
Away from the Via Baltica, petrol stations are scarce, fuel is of poor quality and the possibility of queues always exists. Tankers selling petrol from lay-bys will be seen along main highways.
Leaded: various grades are available, ranging from 75 to 98 octane.
Unleaded : 95 and 98 octane grades available. Quality fuel is available from Neste outlets.
Diesel: central European diesel fuel congeals in winter, and motorists should purchase a special winter diesel with a high congealing point, from Neste and Kesoil stations. Spare fuel: up to 20 litres may be imported.
Payment : Neste service stations accept Visa, Eurocard and Diner's Club. The Neste stations in Latvia accept hard currencies: in Estonia, only Estonian Kroons are acceptable; in Lithuania only Litas are acceptable.

Lighting

In Latvia and Lithuania, mopeds and motorcycles must use dipped headlights at all times. In Estonia, all motor vehicles must use dipped headlights day and night.

Parking

In towns motorists must take care not to park on tram lines. Visitors should be aware that theft of cars and contents is common. Guarded car parks should be used whenever possible.
Estonia: There are a few parking meters in Tallinn and zones where tickets must be pre-paid and displayed on the vehicle. Illegally parked cars will be clamped by the police.
Lithuania: Parking is forbidden within 15m of a bus stop and within 5m of a crossroads or intersection. There are parking spaces in main towns. Clamps are not in use.

Road Networks

The major north-south route linking the Baltic States is the 'Via Baltica' (M12), a hard-surfaced road approximately 620 miles (1000 km) long from Warsawa (Poland) to Tallinn in Estonia. The condition of roads in towns is poor with many potholes. Outside towns the main roads are in good condition but secondary roads are surfaced with gravel or sand.

Night driving

Visitors are not recommended to drive at night. Local drivers tend to use sidelights only, and additional hazards include slow-moving vehicles and obstructions caused by goods falling from vehicles.

Repairs

Spare parts for western makes of car are not available.

Seat belts

The driver and front seat passenger must wear seat belts throughout the Baltic States.

Speed limits

Built-up areas: Estonia and Latvia 30mph (50kmh), Lithuania 37mph (60kmh), outside built-up areas: vehicles up to 3.5 tonnes – normal roads 56mph (90kmh), dual carriageways 68mph (110kmh). Visitors should be aware that fines will be imposed for minor speeding offences.

Temporary importation of vehicles

On arrival in the Baltic States, visitors must sign an undertaking to re-export the vehicle at the end of the stay. The declaration must be shown on leaving the country.

Traffic offences

On-the-spot fines are levied throughout the Baltic States.

Traffic restrictions

Motorists pay an entrance fee to enter the old city of Tallinn, Estonia and the old town of Vilnius, Lithuania.

General information

Accommodation

A range of accommodation is available in the main towns of Vilnius, Kaunas, Tallinn, Riga and Pärnu.

Banks

The following hours are a guide.
Estonia: Mon-Fri 0900-1500/1600
Latvia: Mon-Fri 1000-1430
Lithuania: Mon-Fri 0900-1230 and 1430-1700

Currency

There are no restrictions on the import or export of foreign currency at the time of going to press. Large amounts should be declared on entry to facilitate exportation. The importation and exportation of local currency is prohibited. Visitors are recommended to carry Deutschmarks or US Dollars in small denominations. Visitors are occasionally asked to settle bills in foreign currency. It is an offence to exchange money on the black market.
Estonia: Unit of currency is the Kroon (EEK) divided into 100 centimes. Money can be exchanged at banks, some hotels and the main post office in Tallinn. Credit cards: major cards accepted in Tallinn at major hotels, restaurants and shops.
Latvia: Unit of currency is the Lat, divided into 100 santims. Latvian Roubles are no longer legal tender. Money can be exchanged at banks and some hotels. Credit cards: major cards accepted at some hotels and restaurants.
Lithuania: Unit of currency is the Litas, divided into 100 cents. Exchange money at banks, some hotels and large shops and the main post office in Vilnius. 20 Lita notes are no longer acceptable as means of payment. The Tallon is no longer legal tender. Credit cards: in Vilnius, Visa cards accepted in some shops, restaurants, car hire companies and hotels. Elsewhere credit cards are only accepted in some large hotels and restaurants.

Customs

There are two border crossings from Poland into Lithuania: Ogrodniki, Poland (east of Suwalki) to Lazkijai, Lithuania and Szyplszki, Poland to Kalvarije, Lithuania on the Suwalki to Marijampole Road. Vehicle queues are possible at both crossings caused by local traffic with goods to declare. It is acceptable for motoring visitors to drive past the queue to the border check-point for inspection of vehicle and personal documents by customs officials.

Language

Each country has its national language. Russian is generally understood, but may not be welcome.

Museums

In all countries, museums are usually closed on Monday and in some cases Tuesday as well.

Public holidays

Estonia: New Year's Day; Independence Day, 24 Feb; Good Friday; May Day, 1 May; Victory Day, 23 June; Midsummer's Day, 24 June; Christmas, 25, 26 Dec.
Latvia: New Year's Day; Good Friday; St John's Day, 23 June; National Day, 18 Nov; Christmas, 25, 26 Dec.
Lithuania: New Year's Day; Independence Day, 16 Feb; Restoration of Independence, 11 March; Good Friday; Day of Mourning and Hope, 14 June; National Day, 6 July; All Saint's Day 1 Nov, Christmas, 25, 26 Dec.

Shops

Food shops usually open weekdays 0800-1400 and 1500 to 1700 (1900 or 2000 in Lithuania), Sat 0900-1500 (1800 in Lithuania). In Lithuania, department stores are open Mon-Fri 1000-2000 and Sat 1000-1800.

Visa

Not required by British nationals.

Belgium

Motoring information

National motoring organisation

Royal Automobile Club de Belgique (RACB), FIA, 53 rue d'Arlon, 1040 Bruxelles. Tel: (02) 2870911. Office hours: weekdays 0830–1700.

Accidents and emergencies

Police Tel: 101, Fire Brigade and Ambulance Tel: 100.
When an accident occurs, especially if injuries are involved, police may insist that drivers undergo a blood alcohol content test.
Although in law a driver can refuse, such refusal may result in his arrest.
Belgian law also requires all parties involved in an accident to remain at the scene as long as required by police, and proof of identity may be requested.

Carriage of children

Children under the age of 12 are not permitted on the front seat unless an approved child restraint or child seat is used.

Drinking and driving

The blood alcohol legal limit is 50mg.

Fuel

Most petrol stations are closed overnight from 2000 to 0800, and often all day on Sunday. Petrol stations on motorways and main roads are open 24 hours a day, including Sunday.
Leaded petrol: Super (98/99 octane) available.
Unleaded petrol: Regular (92 octane) and Super (95 octane) available; pump legend *normale sans plomb, normale onglood, normale unverbleit* or *bodvrije benzine*.
Diesel: available.
Credit cards: major cards accepted at most petrol stations on motorways and in large towns.
Spare fuel: 10 litres of petrol in a can may be imported duty free in addition to the fuel in the tank.

Lighting

Use dipped headlights when travelling between dusk and dawn, and when weather conditions are bad. Do not use headlights as parking lights.
Motorcyclists must use dipped headlights during the day.

Orange Badge holders

Orange badge holders may park without time limit in limited time parking zones. Reserved parking is provided for disabled people's vehicles where a white and blue rectangular parking sign is displayed together with a sign showing the disabled person symbol.
Badge holders are exempt from paying at parking meters where local regulations explicitly provide for such payment.

Overtaking

Do not overtake if vehicles are approaching in the opposite direction; or at intersections, unless the road used is marked as a main road or if the traffic is controlled by a policeman or traffic lights; at level crossings; where there is a sign prohibiting overtaking, or if the motorist in front is about to overtake.

Parking

Limited parking zones ('Blue Zones') exist in major cities and towns, where drivers must display a parking disc on their vehicles on weekdays. Signs indicate the entry and exit points of the zone.
Discs are available from the police, garages and certain shops.
Outside a blue zone, a parking disc must be used wherever the parking sign has a panel showing the disc symbol. Elsewhere, paid parking is controlled by parking meters, automatic parking machines and 'cards'.
In the case of meters and machines located within Blue Zones, discs must not be used unless the equipment is out of use.
Do not park within 50 feet (15m) of a bus, tram or trolleybus stop or in the immediate vicinity of train and tram lines crossing the road. Wheel clamps are used on illegally parked vehicles in Antwerpen and Gent.

Priority

Priority must be given to traffic approaching from the right, except when indicated by signs. Do give trams priority over other vehicles.

Signalling

Audible warnings may be used when necessary to indicate your intention to overtake, but only outside built-up areas.

Speed limits

Built-up areas: 31mph (50kmh); outside built-up areas, cars with or without trailer: 56mph (90kmh); motorways: 74mph (120kmh).

Tolls

There are no motorway tolls in Belgium. A toll is charged for the Liefenhoeks Tunnel in Antwerpen.

Traffic offences

Police are empowered to impose and collect on-the-spot fines. For visitors, the fine for a serious offence is 8,000 BF. If the offender refuses to pay, a deposit will be requested. Further non-payment can result in vehicle seizure. Payment is accepted in a number of currencies including £ Sterling.

General information

Banks

Open Mon–Fri 0900–1200 and 1400–1600. Some banks remain open at midday.

Currency

Belgian franc.

Public holidays

New Year's Day; Easter Monday; Labour Day; Ascension; Whit Monday; Flemish National Day, 21 July; Assumption, 15 Aug; All Saints, 1 Nov; Armistice Day, 11 Nov; Christmas, 25 Dec.

Shops

Open 0900–1800 (Fri usually 0900–2100). Some shops close for two hours at midday, but stay open until 2000.

Tourist office

Belgian National Tourist Office, 31 Pepper Street, London, E14 9RW, Tel: 0891-887799 (calls cost 60p per minute at all times).

Bosnia-Herzegovina

At the time of going to print travel is not recommended in Bosnia-Herzegovina.

General information

Embassy

Embassy of the Republic of Bosnia-Herzegovina, 320 Regent Street, London W1R 5AB.
Tel: 0171-255 3758.

Bulgaria

National motoring organisation

Union of Bulgarian Motorists (SBA), FIA, 3 Place Positano, 1090 Sofia. Tel: 2 86 151. Office hours: Mon-Fri 0900-1800.

Accidents and emergencies

Police Tel: 166, Fire Brigade Tel: 160, Ambulance Tel: 150.
In the case of accident, if there is only minor damage to the vehicles, drivers may agree on the procedure to adopt without calling the police. However, if one of the drivers is not insured, the other driver is advised to call the police to draw up a report of the damage which he can produce to his insurance company. If the vehicles are seriously damaged, or if anyone is injured, the police must be called.

Crash helmets

Compulsory for motorcyclists and passengers.

Drinking and driving

Do not drink and drive: blood alcohol legal limit is 0mg.

Fuel

Petrol stations are located in large towns and on main roads, at an average distance of 18-25 miles (30-40km). Some stations are open 24 hours but most open 0600-2130 daily. Motorists should buy fuel from blue pumps.
Leaded petrol: Regular (86 octane) and Super (96 octane) available.
Unleaded petrol: Super (93 octane) available; pump legend *bes olovo bleifrei*.
Diesel: available.
Spare fuel: up to 20 litres of petrol may be imported. Credit cards: accepted at some petrol stations, eg. Shell.

Lighting

In town, drivers must use dipped headlights if public lighting is insufficient. Sidelights may be used in well-lit streets. Foglights may be used only in case of fog, rain or snow, at the same time as sidelights. Dipped headlights should be used if the vehicle is not equipped with foglights.

Orange Badge holders

Parking spaces reserved for disabled drivers are indicated by the sign of the wheelchair. There are no concessions for disabled passengers in private vehicles. Foreign badges are recognised in Bulgaria.

Parking

In built-up areas although there are no parking meters or discs, blue zone parking operates using tickets. Stopping and parking are prohibited at places where they might obstruct traffic. These places are indicated by signs. In one-way streets, parking is on the right only. Outside built-up areas drivers should stop off the road on the hard shoulder and park at places indicated by the international 'P' sign.

Pedestrian crossings

Pedestrians have priority over all vehicles on zebra-type crossings, except trams. When crossing at an intersection, pedestrians already on the carriageway have priority over vehicles, again excepting trams.

Priority

At intersections without right of way, and T junctions, drivers must give way to vehicles coming from the right. Trams have priority over other vehicles approaching from right or left.

Roads

Main roads are numbered, and display international road signs, with distances in kilometres. Town names appear in both Bulgarian and French. There are over 330 miles (530km) of motorways in Bulgaria. The 'Trakia' motorway (156km/96 miles) links the towns of Sofia and Plovdiv.

Seat belts

If fitted, compulsory use in front seats.

Signalling

Audible warning devices (horns) may be used outside large towns to prevent an accident. Places where the use of horns is prohibited are indicated by the international sign.

Speed limits

Built-up areas: motorcycle, car with/without trailer, motorcaravan, 12 seat minibus 30mph (50kmh); outside built-up areas: motorcycle 50mph (80kmh), car with/without trailer, motorcaravan, 12 seat minibus 56mph (90kmh); motorways: motorcycle 62mph (100kmh), car with/without trailer, motorcaravan, 12 seat minibus 74mph (120kmh). All drivers are advised to reduce speed at night on poorly-lit roads. All drivers who have held a driving licence for less than two years must not exceed the following speeds – in built up areas 30mph (50kmh), outside built up areas 44mph (70kmh), motorways 62mph (100kmh).

Tolls

See page 74.

Traffic offences

On-the-spot fines(with receipt) are imposed by police. Minimum fine 200 Leva.

General information

Banks

In Sofia and main towns, usually open Mon-Fri 0800-1230 and 1300-1500, Sat 0800-1400.

Currency

Lev.

Public holidays

New Year's Day; National Day 3 Mar; Easter Mon; Labour Day, 1 May; Education Day, 24 May; Christmas, 25 Dec.

Shops

In Sofia and main towns, usually open Mon-Fri 0800-1700, Sat 0800-1400. Some shops remain open all day.

Visa

A tourist entry visa (valid for three months) is required by British Nationals who arrange their own holiday and stay in Bulgaria for more than 30 hours. For visa application forms, send an sae to: Visa Section, Bulgarian Embassy, 188 Queens Gate, London SW7 5HL or Tel: 0171-584 9400/9433 (Visa section open Mon-Fri 0930-

1230). Seven working days' notice is required. Motorists are recommended to obtain visas in advance of arrival at the border.

Tourist Office

No official tourist office in UK. All enquiries should be made to Balkan Holidays, 19 Conduit Street, London W1R 9TD. Tel: 0171 543 5566 (Customer Services).

CIS

The Commonwealth of Independent States (CIS) comprises Armenia, Azerbaijan, Belarus, Kazakhstan, Kirkghizia, Moldova, Russia, Tajikistan, Turkmenistan, Ukraine and Uzbekistan.

Motoring Information

Accident and breakdown

In the event of accident or breakdown, motorists should obtain assistance from the nearest Intourist office or traffic police. An official accident report (spravka) should be obtained for presentation on leaving the country. Motoring visitors are strongly advised to carry a selection of spare parts for the vehicle as these may not be easily obtainable locally. Purchasers of European Motoring Assistance should consult their Assistance Document.

Drinking and driving

Do not drink and drive: blood alcohol legal limit is 0mg.

Fuel

The standard grade of petrol is 76 octane, however, 95 octane petrol is available at a few outlets. Diesel can sometimes be obtained. Petrol coupons have been discontinued and petrol must now be paid for either in hard currency or roubles. Visitors are advised to carry spare fuel with them as petrol stations are, on average, over 62 miles (100kms) apart. Western brands of oil and anti-freeze are unlikely to be available so a supply should be carried from the UK.

Seat belts

If fitted, compulsory use in front and rear seats.

Speed limits

Built-up areas 37mph (60kmh); outside built-up areas 68mph (110kmh).

Other motoring regulations

Visitors are advised to travel during the day only. When night travel is unavoidable, dipped headlights only should be used. Do not stop in unauthorised places on roads where only transit travel is permitted. The horn should only be used in an emergency. Ensure the vehicle is in good operational order and not driven if a fault could endanger other road users. It is an offence to have a dirty car.

Temporary importation

Motorists considering a visit to the CIS by car are recommended to contact the Consulate for further advice. See under 'Visa' for address.

Travel offences

Traffic police can impose on-the-spot fines for infringement of traffic regulations.

Vehicle insurance

British insurance is not valid in the CIS, and insurance cover may be taken out through the insurance agency (Ingosstrakh) – there are offices in various European countries. Cover may also be obtained on arrival at the frontier posts at Brest (Polish border) and Uzhgorod (Slovakia/Ukraine border).

General information

Currency

Soviet roubles are still the official currency throughout the CIS. Visitors should take US dollars, ideally in small denominations, and should remember that the fluctuating exchange rate can alter prices considerably. Travellers' cheques are not widely accepted.

Language

Away from the main cities, a slight knowledge of the Russian language is beneficial. An ability to read Cyrillic is helpful in order to understand road signs.

Visa

Visas are required by holders of British passports, and are issued by the Consulate of the Russian Federation, 5 Kensington Palace Gardens, London W8, Tel: 0171-229 8027. (The visa section is open 1000-1230, except Wednesdays. Allow 14 working days.) For Ukraine, a visa is available from the Ukraine Embassy, 78 Kensington Park Road, London W11 2PL, Tel: 0171-727 6312. Visas for Uzbekistan and Tajikistan are issued at the border or by the relevant consulate in Moscow.

Croatia

Motoring information

National motoring organisation

Hvratski Auto-Klub, FIA, Draskoviceva 25, 41000 Zagreb. Tel: 41-454 433. Office hours: Mon-Fri 0730-1530 (Tue 1730).

Accidents and emergencies

In the event of an accident, the police must be called. A visitor must obtain a certificate from the police, detailing damage to the vehicle, in order to facilitate export of the vehicle from the country. Police Tel: 92, Fire Brigade Tel: 93, Ambulance Tel: 94.

Carriage of children

Children under 12 must not travel in the front seats.

Crash helmets

Compulsory for motorcyclists, motorcycle passengers and moped riders.

Drinking and driving

Do not drink and drive. The blood alcohol legal limit is 50mg. The Croatian police can carry out breath tests at random.

Fuel

Leaded: Super petrol (98 octane) available. Unleaded 91 and 95 octane grades available. There are approximately 200 stations selling unleaded petrol. Most stations are open 0600-2000. Some of those on major stretches of road stay open 24 hours. Credit cards: some accepted for payment at petrol stations.

Lighting

Spare bulbs must be carried. Motorcyclists must use dipped headlights day and night. Motorists must use dipped headlights when visibility is reduced to 200 metres outside built up areas, and 100 metres inside built up areas, day or night.

Overtaking

Regulations as international practice. Overtake on the left, or on the right if the vehicle to be overtaken is turning left. It is prohibited to overtake a bus transporting children when passengers are getting on or off the bus.

Parking

Lines on the edge of the road indicate a parking prohibition. Traffic wardens control parked vehicles and impose fines for illegal parking.

Priority

Regulations as international practice. At intersections, drivers must give way to traffic from the right unless a priority road is indicated. At roundabouts, vehicles must give way to traffic coming from the right, ie. vehicles entering the roundabout have the right of way. In built up areas, road users must give way to public transport vehicles and to specially marked school buses when these vehicles are leaving a stopping point.

Roads

There are three categories of roads – motorways (300 km), main road (4500 km), and minor roads (7900km). Hrvatski Auto-Klub (HAK) provides road trafffic information 24 hours a day Tel: 041 415 800.

Road signs

Road signs conform to the international pattern.

Seat belts

If fitted, compulsory use in front and rear seats.

Signalling

Do not use horns except in an emergency.

Speed limits

Built-up areas: motorcycle/car/car and caravan or trailer 31mph (50kmh); outside built-up areas: car, motorcycle 56-62mph (90-100kmh); car and trailer 50mph (80kmh); motorways: 81mph (130 kmh); car and caravan or trailer 50mph (80kmh).

Tolls

See page 75.

Traffic lights

The international three-colour system is in use.

Traffic offences

Police are empowered to impose on-the-spot fines for violations of traffic regulations.

General information

Banks

Open Mon-Fri 0800-1900, Sat 0800-1200.

Currency

Croatian kuna. Foreign currency may be exchanged in bureaux de change, banks and post offices. Bureaux de change operate in some hotels and at certain travel agencies. Exchange slips should be kept in order to convert unspent kunas on leaving the country.

Museums

Some museums are closed on Monday and on Sunday afternoon. Information from local tourist office.

Public holidays

New Year's Day; Epiphany 6 Jan; Labour Day 1 May; Constitution Day 30 May; 22 June; Assumption 15 Aug; Christmas 25 and 26 Dec.

Shops

Food shops open Mon-Sat 0600-1930; other shops open Mon-Fri 0800-2000, Sat 0800-1400.

Tourist office

Croatian National Tourist Office, 2 The Lanchesters, 162-164 Fulham Palace Road, London W6 9ER. Tel: 0181 563 7979. Official website: www.htz.hr

Cyprus

Motoring information

National motoring organisation

Cyprus Automobile Association, 12 Chr. Mylonas Street, Nicosia 141. Tel: 02-313233. Office hours: (June-Sep) Mon/Tue/Thu/Fri 0800-1300 and 1500-1900, Wed/Sat 0800-1300.

Accidents and emergencies

Police, Fire Brigade and Ambulance Tel: 199 or 112.

Carriage of children

Children under 10 must not travel in the front seat.

Crash helmets

Recommended.

Drinking and Driving

Suspicion of driving under the influence of alcohol may result in a blood test. Fines imposed. The blood alcohol legal limit is 90mg.

Driving

In Cyprus, drive on the left.

Fuel

Leaded petrol: Regular (87 octane) and Super (98 octane) available.
Unleaded petrol: available in major towns.
Diesel: available.
Spare fuel: it is prohibited to carry fuel in cans.
Credit cards: not accepted.

Lighting

Lights must be used between half an hour after sunset and half an hour before sunrise. Spotlights are prohibited, but foglights may be used.

Priority

As a general rule, give way to vehicles coming from the right. However, traffic on main roads has priority at intersections where a 'Stop' or 'Give Way' sign is placed on the secondary road.

Seat belts

If fitted, compulsory use in front seats.

Signalling

Unnecessary use of the horn is prohibited, particularly from 2200-0600 and near hospitals.

Speed limits

Built-up areas: 31mph (50kmh); outside built-up areas: 50-62mph (80-100kmh).

General information

Banks

Open Mon-Sat 0830-1200, and 1530-1730 for tourists.

Currency

Cypriot pound, which is divided into 100 cents.

Public holidays

New Year; Epiphany, 6 Jan; Greek National Day, 25 Mar; Easter (Greek Orthodox Calendar); National Holiday, 1 Apr; OXI Day, 28 Oct; Christmas, 24-26 Dec.

Shops

Open Mon-Fri 0800-1300 and 1600-1900 (winter 1430-1730), Sat 0800-1300. Shops close Wed afternoons.

Tourist office

Cyprus Tourist Organisation, 213 Regent Street, London, W1R 8DA. Tel: 0171 734 9822.

Czech Republic

Motoring information

National motoring organisations

Ustredni Automotoklub CR (UAMK), FIA , Na Rybnicku 16, 120 76 Praha (Prague) 2. Tel: 2-24 91 18 30. Office hours Mon-Fri 0745-1645.
Autoklub Ceské Republiky (ACR), FIA, Opletalova 29, 110 00 Praha 1. Tel: 2-24 21 02 66. Office hours Mon-Fri 0730-1600.

Accidents and emergencies

Police Tel: 158, Fire Brigade Tel: 150, Ambulance Tel: 155.
If an accident causes bodily injury or material damage exceeding 1,000 Kcs, it must be reported to the police immediately. In the case of accident, where only slight damage occurs it is still advisable to report the accident to police who will issue a certificate to assist in export of vehicle.

Border crossing

All visitors must present their passports at an official border crossing post. However, there are currently no formalities for private cars.

Carriage of children

Children under 12 and less than 150cm in height, are not allowed to travel on the front seat.

Crash helmets

Drivers of motorcycles over 50cc and their passengers must wear crash helmets.

Drinking and driving

Do not drink and drive: blood alcohol legal limit is 0mg.

Fuel

Petrol stations on international roads and in main towns are open 24 hours a day.
Leaded petrol: Regular (91 octane) and Super (96 octane) available.
Unleaded petrol: Super (95 octane) available; pump legend *Natural*. Maps showing outlets for unleaded petrol are issued at border crossings.
Diesel: widely available.

Credit cards: accepted at petrol stations in main towns and tourist areas.

Lighting

Foglights may be used in fog, snow or heavy rain. If the vehicle is not equipped with foglights, the driver must use dipped headlights in these conditions. Motorcyclists must use dipped headlights at all times. While waiting at level crossings, motorists must emit sidelights only.

Orange Badge holders

Holders of parking permits for the disabled (bearing the wheelchair sign) are allowed to park as follows, but they must display the permit in the windscreen:
– for a few minutes on roads where no stopping is allowed
– in short term parking zones in towns, where there is special free parking without time limit for disabled motorists
– in a pedestrian zone, for getting into or out of a vehicle.

Overtaking

Overtaking regulations conform with international usage. In built-up areas, where there are at least two lanes of traffic in each direction, drivers may use either lane. Trams are overtaken on the right. Only when there is no room on the right may the tram be overtaken on the left. In Praha it is prohibited to overtake trams on the left, the driver must follow the tram until he has enough room to pass on the right. Drivers must not overtake beside a tram refuge.

Parking

Vehicles may be parked only on the right of the road. If it is a one-way road, parking is also allowed on the left. Stopping and parking are prohibited in all places where visibility is poor or where the vehicle could cause an obstruction and, in particular, near an intersection, pedestrian crossing, bus or tram stop, level crossing and alongside a tram line unless there is still a 3.5m-wide lane free.
If visiting Praha, it is advisable to park outside the city centre and use public transport. It is forbidden to enter Wenceslas Square (Vacavske namesti) by car, unless you are staying at a hotel in the immediate vicinity. Vehicles illegally parked will be

removed or clamped. Parking meters are being introduced in Praha and Brno.

Priority

At uncontrolled crossroads or road intersections not marked by a priority road sign, priority must be given to vehicles coming from the right. A driver approaching an intersection marked by priority road signs must give right of way to all vehicles approaching this intersection along the priority road.
Drivers may not enter crossroads unless their exit beyond the intersection is clear. A tram turning right and crossing the line of a vehicle on its right has priority.

Road signs

Most conform to the international pattern. Other road signs which may be seen are:
chodte vlevo: pedestrians must walk on the left
dalkovy provov: bypass
h nemocnice: hospital
jednosmerny provoz: one-way traffic
obji zdka: diversion
prujezd zakázáb: closed to all vehicles

Seat belts

If fitted, compulsory use in front and rear seats.

Signalling

Horns may be used only to warn other road users in case of danger or to signify that you are going to overtake. Warning may also be given by flashing the headlights. The use of horns is prohibited in central Praha 2100-0500 from 15 March to 15 October and 2000-0600 from 15 October to 15 March.

Speed limits

Built-up areas: 37mph (60kmh); outside built-up areas: 56mph (90kmh); motorways: 81mph (130kmh). Cars with caravan-trailer 50mph (80kmh).

Tolls

See page 75.

Traffic offences

On-the-spot fines of up to 2000 Kc in cash or 7000 Kc to be paid later may be imposed.

General information

Banks

Open Mon-Fri 0830-1630. Closed Sat.

Currency

Czech crown ('Koruna 'ceska' Kc).

Museums

Open Tue-Sat 1000-1700. Closed Mon.

Castles

Castles are usually open from 1 May to 31 August. Open Tue-Sat, 1000-1600/1800. Closed Mon.

Personal safety

Visitors to Praha should be aware of the high incidence of petty theft. Pickpockets operate at the main tourist attractions, particularly the Charles Bridge, Prague Castle, Wenceslas Square, Old Town Square and the Jewish Cemetary. Theft occurs frequently on trains, trams and at the main railway station. Passports and valuables should be left in a hotel safe. Carry small quantities of cash and a photocopy of your passport for identification purposes.

Public holidays

New Year's Day; Easter Monday; May Day; National Liberation Day, 8 May; St Cyril and St Method, 5 July; Johannes Hus Festival Day, 6 July; Independence Day, 28 October; Christmas 24-26 Dec.

Shops

Food shops open Mon-Fri 0800-1800, Sat 0800-1200. Department stores open Mon-Fri 0800/0900-1900 (Thu 2000), Sat 0800-1500.

Visa

British Nationals no longer require a visa.

Tourist office

Czech Tourist Office, Czech Centre, 95 Great Portland Street, London W1N 5RA. Tel: 0171 291 9925.

Denmark

Motoring information

National motoring organisation

No FIA affiliated club.

Accidents and emergencies

Police, Fire Brigade and Ambulance Tel: 112.

Carriage of children

Children under three must be seated in a restraint system adapted to their size. Children over three may use a child restraint instead of a seat belt. Use of seat belts can be combined with use of a booster cushion.

Crash helmets

Compulsory for motorcyclists and passengers.

Drinking and driving

The blood alcohol legal limit is 50mg.

Fuel

Fuel availability is limited on motorways, and motorists are advised to fill their tank before joining a motorway.
Petrol stations are often closed at night other than in large towns. There is an increasing number of self-service stations open 24 hours with pumps that require 100 DKK notes.
Leaded petrol: Super (98 octane) available.
Unleaded petrol: Regular (92 octane), Super (95 and 98 octane) available.
Diesel: available
Credit cards: major cards accepted at larger petrol stations.
Spare fuel: a full can may be imported if entering from an EU country.

Internal ferries

Car ferries link the north Jutland peninsula with the island of Zealand and the Danish capital, København.
A frequent car ferry service operates from Puttgarden, Germany to Rødby, Denmark providing road and bridge connections to København.

A leaflet on international and internal ferry services is available from the Danish Tourist Board.

Level crossings

Drivers must reduce speed when approaching level crossings. Side lights only should be used at night when waiting at level crossings.

Lighting

Dipped headlamps must be used at all times.

Mirrors

Right-hand drive vehicles must be equipped with exterior side mirrors on both sides.

Motorways

No tolls are levied on the 400 mile (650km) motorway network in Denmark.
Service areas, open from 0700–2200, are located at 30 mile (50km) intervals providing toilet, cafeteria facilities and travel information.
Petrol stations are sited at similar intervals, on or just off the motorway, some have a cafeteria and shop. They are generally open 0700–2200 with automatic pumps for overnight use.
Lay-bys are also located along motorways but do not have toilet facilities.

Orange Badge holders

Disabled motorists displaying their badge in the windscreen may park for up to 15 minutes where only loading/unloading is permitted, where parking is prohibited or in parts of pedestrian areas where delivery vehicles are allowed.
Parking for up to one hour is allowed where normally 15 or 30 minutes is permitted.
Unlimited parking is allowed where 1, 2 or 3 hours is permitted or at parking meters or car parks with coin machines, providing the maximum amount is paid on arrival. In each case the arrival time must be set on the parking disk.

Parking

In central København, in addition to restrictions indicated by signs, parking discs are required where there are no parking meters.
Disc parking is usually restricted to one hour.
At meters, parking is allowed for up to three hours. They are in use weekdays 0900–1800 and on Saturdays 0900–1300. 1 Kr and 25 Ore coins are used.

In other large towns, kerbside parking is usually restricted to one hour.
Discs are available from tourist offices, banks, post offices, petrol stations, and FDM offices.
Do not park where there is a sign *Parkering forbudt*, or stop where signed *Stopforbudt*.
Unlawful parking will result in the police towing the vehicle away. The vehicle will be released only upon payment of a fine.

Priority

Give way to traffic from the right except at roundabouts, where traffic already on the roundabout has priority.
Do give way to traffic on a major road at a line of triangles painted across the carriageway or at a triangular 'Give Way' sign, and also to buses.
Do not turn right at a red light, even if the road is clear, unless a green arrow indicates that you may.
At junctions give way to cyclists and motorcyclists moving ahead when you are turning.
When turning right, watch out for cyclists approaching from behind.

Road signs

Most conform to the international pattern. Other road signs are:

  Ensrettet kørsel: one-way street
  Fare: danger
  Farligt sving: dangerous bend
  Fodgaengerovergang: pedestrian crossing
  Gennemkørsel forbudt: no through road
  Hold til højre: keep to the right
  Hold till venstre: keep to the left
  Indkørsel forbudt: no entry
  Korsvej: crossroads
  Omkørsel: diversion
  Parkering forbudt: no parking
  Vejarbejde: road up
  Vejen er spaerret: road closed

Signalling

Do not use your horn except in case of danger.
Flash your lights instead.

Speed limits

Built-up areas: 31mph (50kmh); outside built-up areas: 50mph (80kmh); motorways: 68mph (110kmh); cars towing a caravan or trailer 44mph (70kmh).

Tolls

The Storebaeltsbroen (Great Belt Link) comprises a road bridge and rail tunnel link between the islands of Funen and Zealand. See page 75 for toll charges.

Traffic offences

Danish police are authorised to impose and collect on-the-spot fines.
If the visitor does not accept the fine, the case will be taken to court. The vehicle can be impounded until the matter is resolved and fines paid.

General information

Banks

Open Mon–Wed, Fri 0930–1600, Thu 0930–1800, closed Sat.

Currency

Kroner.

Medical treatment

Medical pharmacies are called *Apotek* and in Danish towns a number of these operate a 24-hour service.

Public holidays

New Year's Day; Maundy Thursday; Good Friday; Easter Monday; Constitution Day, 5 June; Ascension; Whit Monday; Christmas 24, 25, 26 and 31 Dec.

Shops

København: open Mon–Thu 0900–1730, Fri 0900–1900/2000, Sat 0900–1300/1400.
Provinces: open Mon–Thu 0900–1730, Fri 0900–1730/1900, Sat 0900–1200/1300. Larger stores: open Mon–Fri 0900–1800/1900, Sat 0900–1200/1400.

Tourist office

Danish Tourist Board, 55 Sloane Street, London SW1X 9SY, Tel: 0171-259 5959
Official website: www.dtb.dt.dk

Finland

Motoring information

National motoring organisation

Autoliitto Automobile and Touring-Club of Finland (AL), FIA, Hämeentie 105, 00550 Helsinki 0050. Tel: 9-774 761. Office hours: Mon 0830–1730, Tue–Fri 0830 1600.

Accidents and emergencies

Police Tel: 10022, Fire Brigade and Ambulance Tel: 112. If you have an accident, report it to the Finnish Motor Insurance Bureau: Liikennevakuutusyhdistys, Bulevardi 28, 00120 Helsinki 12, Tel: (9) 019251.

Carriage of children

Children must be restrained either with a seat belt or in a child seat.

Drinking and driving

The blood alcohol legal limit is 50mg.

Fuel

Petrol stations are usually open 0700–2100 weekdays, shorter hours at weekends. Some petrol stations are open 24 hours. There are automatic pumps which operate upon insertion of bank notes.
Leaded petrol has been withdrawn from sale at certain outlets and replaced with an unleaded petrol grade containing special additive. Unleaded petrol: Regular (95 octane) and Super (98 octane) available; pump legend *ljyton polttaine*.
Diesel: available.
Credit cards: accepted at most petrol stations. Spare fuel: there is no limit on the amount of fuel imported by visitors from other EU countries provided it is for personal use.

Orange Badge holders

Orange badge holders should present their permit to the local police in order to apply for a Finnish parking permit, which should then be displayed in their vehicle windscreen. Badge holders granted a permit can park free of charge in a space where parking is subject to payment and in an area where parking is prohibited by blue and red no waiting and white and blue parking signs, provided other traffic regulations do not hinder it. These concessions apply only to the vehicle stated on the permit.

Lighting

Outside built-up areas all motor vehicles must use their headlights at all times.

Overtaking

Overtake on the left, unless the vehicle to be overtaken is signalling to turn left. In parallel lines of traffic, vehicles may be overtaken on the right. Vehicles being overtaken should not cross the white line which indicates the lane for cyclists and pedestrians.

Parking

Stopping and parking prohibitions follow international practice.
Parking meters are usually grey and operate for between 15 minutes and four hours. Parking lights must be used if the parking place is not sufficiently lit. Although wheel clamps are not in use, police may remove illegally parked vehicles, and levy a fine.

Priority

At intersections, vehicles coming from the right have priority except on main roads. The approach to these main roads is indicated by a sign with a red triangle on a yellow background. When this sign is supplemented by a red octagon with 'STOP' in the centre of the sign, vehicles must stop before entering the intersection. Trams and emergency vehicles, even when coming from the left, always have priority over other vehicles.

Road signs

Most signs conform to international pattern. Others include:
Lossi-farja: ferry
Tulli: customs
Aja hitaasti: drive slowly
Tie rakenteilla: road under construction
Päällystetyötä: road resurfacing
Kunnossapitotyö: road repairs
Aluerajoitus: local speed limit

France

Signalling

It is prohibited to sound a horn in towns and villages except in cases of immediate danger. Outside built-up areas horns and headlights should be used when and wherever visibility is not perfect.

Speed limits

Built-up areas: 31mph (50kmh); outside built-up areas: 50–62mph (80–100kmh); motorways: 74mph (120kmh); cars towing a caravan or trailer: 50mph (80kmh).

Traffic offences

Police are empowered to impose on-the-spot fines but not authorised to collect them. Payment of fines must be made at a post office within 2 weeks. Minimum fine – 150 FIM.

General information

Banks

Open Mon–Fri 0915–1615. Exchange offices are open longer hours, especially at Helsinki airport and ports.

Currency

Markka (FIM or Finnish mark).

Public holidays

New Year's Day; Epiphany; Good Friday; Easter Monday; May Day; first Sat after Ascension; Whit Saturday; All Saints, first Sat in Nov; Independence Day, 6 Dec; Christmas Day; St Stephen's Day. Other days are Vappu night, 30 Apr (a student and spring festival). Midsummer, 24 June is celebrated throughout Finland on the Saturday nearest to 24 June with bonfires and dancing.

Shops

Open Mon–Fri 0900–1700, Sat 0900–1400/1600 according to season, and there are local variations.
Shops at Helsinki railway and Metro stations are open Mon–Sat 1000–2200, Sun 1200–2200.

Tourist office

Finnish Tourist Board, 30–35 Pall Mall, London SW1Y 5LP, Tel: 0171-839 4048
Official website: www.finland-tourism.com

Motoring information

National motoring organisations

Automobile Club de France, FIA, 6–8 Place de la Concorde, 75008 Paris. Tel: 1-43 12 43 12. Office hours: Mon–Fri 0900–1800.
Automobile Club National (ACN), FIA, 5 rue Auber, 75009 Paris. Tel: 1-44 51 53 99. Office hours: Mon–Thurs 0900–1300 and 1400–1800 (Fri 1700).

Accidents and emergencies

Police Tel: 17, Fire Brigade Tel: 18. Ambulance Tel: 15.

Breakdowns

Orange emergency telephones are situated every 2km along autoroutes and main roads.

Carriage of children

Children under 10 years of age must be seated on the rear seat of the car and use seat belts or child seat safety restraints adapted to their size. The only exception to this are babies or a very young child using approved rear-facing child seats.

Documents

The French police can ask to see the vehicle registration document and driving licence. Motorists unable to produce documents immediately are liable to a 75F fine. If they are not presented at a police station within 5 days, a further 900F fine is liable.

Drinking and driving

The blood alcohol legal limit is 50mg.

Fuel

Leaded petrol: Super (98 octane) available. Unleaded petrol: Super (95/98 octane) available; pump legend *essence sans plomb*. Diesel: sold at pumps marked *gas-oil* or *gaz-oil*. Credit cards: major credit cards accepted. Spare fuel: up to 10 litres of spare fuel may be imported in cans.

Internal ferries

Car ferry services operate across the Gironde estuary between Royan and Le Verdon, and in the south between Blaye and Lamasque. Crossing time is 30 minutes and 25 minutes respectively. Services operate during daylight hours throughout the year.

Lighting

Headlight beams must be adjusted for right-hand drive vehicles. Beam converter sets, which can be fitted quickly and easily, are obtainable from RAC. There is now no legal requirement for vehicles to emit a yellow beam.

It is compulsory to use headlights at night in all areas, but these must be dipped in built-up areas. Motorcycle headlights are compulsory, day and night.

Do use headlights in poor visibility. Parking lights are obligatory, unless public lighting is sufficient for the vehicle to be seen distinctly from an adequate distance. A single offside parking light is permissible, provided the light is illuminated on the side nearest the traffic.

If a driver 'flashes' you, he expects you to pull to one side and let him pass.

Visiting motorists are recommended to carry a set of spare bulbs for the front lights, rear lights, stop lights and direction indicator lights.

Orange Badge holders

Local authorities are responsible for parking concessions. There are no general street parking concessions, apart from reserved spaces for people with disabilities (indicated by the international symbol). However, police must show consideration for parking by identifiable disabled people's vehicles, providing they are not causing an obstruction.

Concessions vary from town to town it is worth enquiring locally if there are any available.

Overloading

The French authorities are concerned by the serious overloading of many British-registered cars which are touring in France.

Apart from the possible danger to all passengers, if involved in an accident the driver could well be prosecuted or held responsible for the accident by carrying more passengers and/or excessive weight than the vehicle manufacturer recommends.

Overtaking

Do not overtake where the road is marked with one or two continuous unbroken lines or when a vehicle is already being overtaken, or when a tram is stationary with passengers alighting or boarding.

Processions, funerals or troops must not be overtaken at over 18mph.

You may overtake, giving the correct signal, where the road is marked by broken lines, although the line may only be crossed for the time taken to pass.

A tram in motion may be overtaken on the right only, but on the left in a one-way street if there is sufficient space.

Parking

The usual restrictions on parking operate as in the UK with the following additions:

(a) Do not park where the kerbs are marked with yellow paint or where you will cause an obstruction.

(b) On roads outside town limits you must pull off the highway. Unilateral parking on alternate days is indicated by signs *Coté du Stationnement*, *jours pairs* – even (or *impairs* – odd).

In narrow streets in Paris, where parking both sides would obstruct the passage of double line traffic, this regulation applies automatically.

Parking is prohibited in Paris along two main access routes – *axes rouges* (red routes). The east-west route includes the left banks of the Seine and the Quai de la Mégisserie; the north-south route includes the Avenue du Général Leclerc, part of the Boulevard St Michel, the rue de Rivoli, boulevards Sébastopol, Strasbourg, Barbès, Ornano, rue Lafayette and Avenue Jean Jaurès.

Do not leave a parked vehicle in the same place in Paris for more than 24 consecutive hours. This restriction also applies in Hauts-de-Seine, Seine-St Denis and Val de Marne.

In Paris and the larger cities, there are Blue Zones, where parking discs must be used. They may be obtained from police stations, tourist offices and some shops.

When a kerbside space has been found, the disc must be displayed on the windscreen and the

clock set showing both the time of arrival and when the parking space will be free. Parking is limited to 1 hour 30 mins 0900–1900 (except between 1130 and 1430).
Discs are not required on Sundays and public holidays.
In other places, parking is shown by the international parking signs on which particular regulations are shown in black letters on a white background.
In some towns and cities, parking discs have been replaced with meters and pay and display schemes (*horodateurs*).
In Paris and some other large towns, illegally parked vehicles will be clamped or towed away. The vehicle will be released only upon payment of a fine.

Priority

The *priorité à droite* for all roads no longer holds. Traffic on major roads now has priority.
Where two major roads cross, the sign *Danger Priorité à Droite* is used, indicating that traffic coming from the right has priority.
Passage protégé (priority road) signs indicate those major roads where traffic has priority. In the absence of signs, give way to traffic from the right.
Since 1984 traffic already on a roundabout has priority, and a triangular sign with a red border showing a roundabout symbol with the legend *vous n'avez pas la priorité* indicates this. However, in a few areas the old ruling of priority given to traffic entering the roundabout still applies. So, where the signs are not present, you should approach with care.

Road signs

Conform to the international pattern but other road signs are:
  Allumez vos lanternes: switch on your lights
  Attention au feu: fire hazard
  Attention travaux: beware roadworks
  Barrière de dégel: applies to lorries when ice is thawing and roads are closed to lorries to prevent deterioration of road surface
  Chaussée déformée: uneven road surface
  Fin d'interdiction de stationner: end of prohibited parking

  Gravillons: loose chippings
  Haute tension: electrified line
  Interdit aux piétons: forbidden to pedestrians
  Nids de poules: potholes
  Rappel: remember (displayed on speed limit signs)
  Route barrée: road closed

Signalling

Do not use horns except in an emergency.

Speed limits

Motorcycles over 80cc, private cars, vehicles towing a caravan or trailer with total weight under 3.5 tonnes: in built-up areas the speed limit is 31mph (50kmh), but this can be raised to 44mph (70kmh) on important through roads as indicated by signs; outside built-up areas on normal roads 56mph (90kmh); priority roads and toll free urban motorways 68mph (110kmh); toll motorways 81mph (130kmh).
Cars towing a caravan or trailer with total weight exceeding 3.5 tonnes: outside built-up areas the speed limit is 50mph (80kmh) on normal roads; priority roads 50mph (80kmh), but increased to 62mph (100kmh) on dual carriageways and to 68mph (110kmh) on motorways. Special speed limits apply if the trailer weight is more than the towing vehicle.
On the Paris Périphérique ring road the speed limit is 50mph (80kmh).
A minimum speed limit of 50mph (80kmh) applies for vehicles in the left lane of motorways.
In rain and bad weather, speed limits are lowered to: motorways 68mph (110kmh); dual carriageways 62mph (100kmh); other roads outside built-up areas 50mph (80kmh).
Visitors who have held a licence for less than two years are limited to 50mph (80kmh) on normal roads; 62mph (100kmh) on urban motorways and 68mph (110kmh) on toll motorways.
The speed limit does not have to be displayed on the vehicle.

Tolls

Payable on the autoroute network (see page 75). Tolls are also payable on the following bridges:
  from the mainland (west coast) onto Ile de Ré and Ile de Noirmoutier;
  Pont de Martrou, Rochefort (Charente Maritime);

Pont de St Nazaire (Loire Atlantique);
Pont de Brotonne (Seine Maritime).

Traffic lights

As in Britain except there is no amber light after the red light. Flashing amber means proceed with caution. Flashing red means no entry. Flashing yellow arrows mean the drivers may proceed in direction indicated, but must give way to pedestrians and the traffic flow they are joining.

Traffic offences

Some French police are authorised to impose and collect fines of up to 2,500F on the spot from drivers who violate traffic regulations. An official receipt should be requested.
If a minor offence is committed, a reduced fine is payable within 30 days.
A court hearing must be arranged if the fine is to be contested.
A guarantee must be deposited if a serious offence is committed by a non-resident which is likely to result in a heavy fine and suspension of driving licence or prison sentence.

General information

Banks

Open weekdays 0900–1200 and 1400–1600. Some provincial banks open Tue-Sat 0900–1200 and 1400–1600.

Currency

French franc.

Museums

Most museums are closed Monday.

Public holidays

New Year's Day; Easter Monday; Labour Day; VE Day, 8 May; Ascension; Whit Monday; Bastille Day, 14 July; Assumption, 15 Aug; All Saints, 1 Nov; Armistice Day, 11 Nov; Christmas, 25 Dec.

Shops

Shops are often closed on Mon, all or half day, and for lunch two hours each day. Food shops are open Sunday morning.

Tourist office

Maison de la France (French Tourist Office), 178 Piccadilly, London W1V 0AL, Tel: 0891-244123 (calls cost 60p per minute at all times). Official website: www.franceguide.com

Germany

Motoring information

National motoring organisations

Allgemeiner Deutscher Automobil-Club (ADAC), FIA, Am Westpark 8, 81373 München. Tel: (089) 76760. 24-hour information service, Tel: (089) 22222. Office hours: weekdays 0800–1700, Sat ADAC District Offices in main towns open 0800–1200.
Automobil-Club von Deutschland (AVD), FIA, Lyonerstrasse 16, 60528 Frankfurt-am-Main. Tel: (069) 6606-0. Office hours: weekdays 0800–1700.

Accidents and emergencies

Police, Fire Brigade, Ambulance: generally 112 in most areas.

Breakdowns

Both the motoring clubs (above) maintain emergency patrol services on motorways and main routes.

Carriage of children

Children under 12 and children of less than 1.50m in height may only travel on seats that are fitted with a child restraint system.
Travel on rear seats is permitted without restraint when all available restraints are in use. (A fine of 40 DM can be imposed if this is not observed)

Drinking and driving

The blood alcohol legal limit is 50mg.

Fuel

Leaded petrol: no longer available, lead substitute additive can be bought and added to fuel for those cars unable to use unleaded petrol.
Unleaded petrol: Regular (91 octane) and Super

(95/98 octane) available; pump legend *bleifrei normal* or *bleifrei super*.
Diesel: available.
Credit cards: accepted at most petrol stations.
Spare fuel: a full can of fuel may be imported duty free for use by vehicles registered in an EU country.

Lighting

When visibility is reduced by rain, fog or snow, use dipped headlights – driving with sidelights only is prohibited. Auxiliary/foglights should be used only with dipped headlights, even in daylight.
Motorcyclists are advised to use headlights at all times.

Motorways

There are no tolls payable on autobahns.
Fuel, restaurant and accommodation facilities, usually open 24 hours, are widely available on the network.

Orange Badge holders

Orange badge holders are allowed to park as follows:
– a maximum of 3 hours where a blue and red no waiting sign is displayed and in parking areas reserved for residents (arrival time must be shown on permit)
– beyond the permitted time in areas covered by a parking or no waiting sign
– beyond the permitted time where a white and blue rectangular parking sign is displayed or where the parking period is restricted by a supplementary sign in a street parking area
– during permitted periods for loading/unloading in pedestrian zones
– without charge or time limit at parking meters unless other parking facilities are available within a reasonable distance.

Overtaking

Do not overtake when passengers are boarding or alighting from a bus or tram. Do not overtake a tram if there is insufficient room on the right.
In one-way streets trams can be overtaken on either side, but normally on the right when in motion. You must indicate your intention when overtaking or changing lanes. In urban areas there is free choice of traffic lane if several lanes are available.

It is prohibited to overtake or pass a school bus, which has stopped outside a built-up area, when red lights are flashing.

Parking

Except for one-way streets, parking is only permitted on the right side unless loading, boarding, or unloading.
Do not park on roads with priority road signs, or where it would be dangerous to other traffic or pedestrians, outside built-up areas. Both meters and parking disc zones are in use.

Pedestrian crossings

Do give a pedestrian absolute priority on all pedestrian crossings, which are indicated on the road by white bands 50cm wide.

Priority

At the junction of two main roads or two minor roads, traffic from the right has priority, unless the contrary is indicated.
Main road traffic has priority and that travelling on motorways has priority over vehicles entering or leaving. Vehicles turning left at an intersection must give way to all oncoming vehicles.
Trams do not have priority; buses do have priority when leaving bus stops.
You must give way to a bus driver who has signalled his intention to leave the kerb.

Road signs

Most conform to the international pattern. Other road signs which may be seen are:
Autobahn kreuz: motorway junction
Baustofflagerung: roadworks material
Einbahnstrasse: one-way street
Fahrbahnwechsel: change traffic lane
Frostschäden: frost damage
Glatteisgefahr: ice on the road
Radweg kreuzt: cycle track crossing
Rollsplitt: loose grit
Seitenstreifen nicht bafahrbar: use of verge not advised
STAU: slow-moving traffic – drive with care
Strassenschäden: road damage
Umleitung: diversion

Signalling

Do not sound your horn unnecessarily; this is forbidden. Outside built-up areas audible warning may be given if the driver intends to overtake another vehicle. At night, drivers must give warning of their approach by flashing their headlights.

Speed limits

Built-up areas: 31mph (50kmh); outside built-up areas: 62mph (100kmh); on motorways, the recommended maximum is 81mph (130kmh). These speed limits also apply in the five federal states (these were formerly East Germany). Cars towing a caravan or trailer are limited to 50mph (80kmh) on all roads outside built-up areas. There is a minimum speed of 37mph (60kmh) on motorways and expressways. When visibility is below 50 metres, the maximum speed limit is 31mph (50kmh) on all roads.

Traffic lights

The international three-colour system is used throughout Germany. A red light with a green filter arrow pointing to the right permits a right turn, however, motorists must give way to other road users and pedestrians.

Traffic offences

The German police are empowered to impose and collect on-the-spot fines of up to 75 DM. Motorists may pay the fine during the course of the following week. In cases of speed limit violations, a sliding scale of fines operates. A visitor can be asked to deposit a sum of money, and if he refuses or cannot pay, the vehicle may be impounded.

General information

Banks

Open Mon–Fri 0830–1230 and 1330–1430 (Thu 1730). Closed Sat.

Currency

Deutschmark.

Public holidays

New Year's Day; Good Friday; Easter Monday; Labour Day; Ascension; Whit Monday; Day of Unity, 17 June; Unification Day, 3 Oct; Christmas, 25, 26 Dec. In addition, some areas observe Epiphany, Corpus Christi, Assumption, All Saints and Repentance days.

Shops

Open Mon–Fri 0830/0900–1800/1830. Close Sat at 1400.

Tourist office

German National Tourist Office, PO Box 2695, London, W1A 3TN, Tel: 0891-600100 (calls cost 60p per minute at all times).
Official website: www.germany-tourism.de

Gibraltar

Motoring information

National motoring organisation

RAC Agent: A M Capurro and Sons Ltd, 20 Line Wall Road, Gibraltar. Tel: 75149.

Caravans and camping

The temporary importation of trailer caravans and motor caravans is prohibited, although Customs may grant an exception provided the owner is a bona fide visitor and does not intend to use the vehicle for camping purposes.

Crash helmets

Compulsory for motorcyclists and passengers on machines over 50cc.

Accidents and emergencies

Police Tel: 190, Fire Brigade and Ambulance Tel: 199.

Fuel

Leaded petrol: Super (98 octane) available.
Unleaded petrol: Super (95 octane) available.
Diesel: available.

Credit cards: not accepted. Spare fuel: 20 gallons may be imported in a sealed steel container. It must be declared to Customs, and duty is payable.

Lighting

You must drive with dipped headlights at night.

Parking

Car parks are at Grand Parade (near lower cable car station), at Eastern Beach, Catalan Bay and at Casemates Square. Street parking is allowed in Queensway, Line Wall Road, Devils Tower Road and Rosia Road. Much of the town centre is pedestrianised, so motorists should park outside the city walls.
Vehicles parked in restricted areas will be towed away or immobilised.
If this occurs the driver should go to the Central Police Station in Irish Town. Parking areas are clearly marked.

Priority

Vehicles already on a roundabout have priority.

Roads

On the Upper Rock, roads are narrow, winding and steep. Signposts indicate those roads not open to civilian traffic. Visitors are therefore recommended to take a Rock Tour by taxi or minicoach.

Speed limits

Maximum 25mph (40kmh). Lower limits are signposted.

General information

Banks

Open Mon–Thu 0900–1530 (Fri some open 0900–1800).

Border crossing

Motorists should beware of civilians illegally selling tickets for the border crossing.

Public holidays

New Year's Day; Commonwealth Day, 13 Mar; Easter; May Day; Spring Bank Holiday; Queen's Birthday; Late Summer Bank Holiday; Christmas.

Shops

Open Mon–Fri 0900–1700, Sat 0900–1300.

Tourist office

Gibraltar Information Bureau, Arundel Great Court, 179 The Strand, London WC2R 1EH, Tel: 0171-836 0777
Official website: www.gibraltar.gi

Greece

Motoring information

National motoring organisation

The Automobile and Touring Club of Greece (ELPA), FIA, 2–4 Messogion Street, (Athens Tower), 115 27 Athína (Athens). Tel: 748 8800. Office hours: Mon–Fri 0830–1930, Sat 0830–1330.

Accidents and emergencies

Police Tel: 100 (Athína, Pireás, Thessaloníki, Pátrai, Corfu), 109 (suburbs of Athína); Fire Brigade Tel: 199, Ambulance Tel: 166 (Athína) – for other towns see local directory.

Breakdowns

ELPA's road assistance service (OVELPA) operates on a 24-hour basis and covers all main roads, as well as the islands of Crete and Corfu. For assistance Tel: 104.

Carriage of children

It is prohibited for children under the age of 10 to travel in the front seat.

Drinking and driving

The blood alcohol legal limit is 50mg.

Fuel

Leaded petrol: Regular (91/92 octane) and Super (98 octane) available.
Unleaded petrol: Super (95/98 octane) available; pump legend *amoliwdi wensina*.
Diesel: available.
Credit cards: accepted at some petrol stations.
Spare fuel: it is prohibited to import fuel in cans.

Lighting

Do not use undipped headlights in towns. A motor vehicle parked at night on a public road must have the rear red light clearly illuminated.

Overtaking

Overtaking is prohibited when approaching an unguarded level crossing.

Parking

The usual restrictions apply. Some streets have only unilateral parking, or impose a 30-minute limit. In Athína you may park only at meters although special parking sites are available to visitors. Caravans are also admitted for parking. The police will remove your registration plates if you stop or park in a no-parking zone. This practice applies also in some areas outside Athína. Greek-registered vehicles have been banned from a zone in the centre of Athína on certain days. Visiting motorists are exempted if their stay in Greece does not exceed 40 days.

Priority

In towns priority must be accorded to traffic entering from the right. In the open country, main road traffic has priority.

Road signs

International road signs are in use.

Signalling

Your warning device must be of low-pitched regular tone. Multitone sirens, klaxons, whistles and hooters are all forbidden. The horn may be used in open country, but in towns it is allowed only in an emergency.

Speed limits

Built-up areas: motorcycles 25mph (40kmh); car with or without caravan/trailer 31mph (50kmh); outside built-up areas: motorcycles 44mph (70kmh), car with or without caravan/trailer 68mph (110kmh); motorways and national roads: motorcycles 56mph (90kmh), car with or without caravan/trailer 75mph (120kmh).

Tolls

See page 77

Traffic offences

Fines imposed by the Greek police are payable to the Public Treasury, not to a police officer.

General information

Banks

Open Mon–Fri 0800–1400 in major tourist areas. Foreign exchange counters often open again in the afternoon and evening.

Currency

Drachma.

Public holidays

New Year's Day; Epiphany; Independence Day, 25 Mar; Shrove Monday; Good Friday; Easter Monday; Labour Day; Whit Monday; Assumption, 15 Aug; Ohi Day (National Day), 28 Oct; Christmas, 25, 26 Dec.

Shops

Usually open Mon 0930–1900, Tue–Fri 0900–1900, Saturday 0900–1530.

Tourist office

Hellenic National Tourism Organisation, 4 Conduit Street, London W1R 0DJ, Tel: 0171-734 5997.

Hungary

Motoring information

National motoring organisation

Magyar Autóklub (MAK), FIA , Rómer Flóris utca 4/a, Budapest II. Tel: 1-212 2938. Office hours: Mon-Thu 0730-1600, Fri 0730-1500. Closed Sat.

Accidents and emergencies

Police Tel: 107, Fire Brigade Tel: 105, Ambulance Tel: 104. Accidents causing damage or injury to persons must be reported to the nearest policeman or police station (Tel: Budapest 107) and to the Hungarian State Insurance Company (Hungaria Biztosító) within 24 hours. The police will issue a statement, which the motorist must show when leaving Hungary, in order to avoid lengthy delays at the frontier.

Carriage of children

Children less than 150cm in height, are not allowed to travel on the front seat unless the vehicle has a child restraint seat.

Crash helmets

Compulsory for motorcyclists and passengers on machines over 50cc which can exceed 50kmh.

Drinking and driving

The blood alcohol legal limit is 0mg.

Fuel

On motorways and in large towns, petrol stations are open 24 hours. Otherwise, hours are 0600-2000.
Leaded petrol: 98 octane available.
Unleaded petrol: Regular (91 octane) and Super (95/98 octane) available; pump legend *olommentes uzemanyag*. Availability is indicated by a white sign with blue border and an illustration of two pumps – black (leaded) and green (unleaded). Diesel: visiting motorists are recommended to fill their tanks at SHELL or AFOR stations to avoid inferior fuel on sale at some filling stations. Credit cards: Eurocard accepted at some petrol stations. Spare fuel: it is prohibited to import or export fuel in cans. Coupons: the coupon scheme has been discontinued.

Lighting

Outside built-up areas, including motorways, dipped headlights must be used day and night. In built-up areas at night, the use of full headlights is prohibited, and dipped headlights must be used. A spare set of bulbs must be carried by residents only.

Motorways

Emergency telephones are located at 2km intervals on motorways. Catering facilities are usually located near petrol stations. Motel accommodation is rarely available on motorways.

Orange Badge holders

There are parking spaces reserved for disabled motorists. These are indicated by the international sign of the wheelchair.

Overtaking

Vehicles must overtake on the left. On roads where tram-rails are placed in the middle of the road, a moving tram or vehicle signalling its intention to turn left must be overtaken on the right.

Parking

To reduce traffic congestion and pollution, the centre of Budapest is closed to private traffic. On two-way roads vehicles must be parked on the right-hand side of the road, facing in the direction of the traffic. They may be parked on either side of one-way roads. Do not park in places where you would not park in Britain.

Pedestrian crossings

Pedestrians have right of way at pedestrian crossings and priority at intersections over turning traffic. They do not have priority on the roadway between tramloading islands and the kerb. Drivers must show special care on these sections.

Priority

Major roads are indicated by a priority road ahead sign. At the intersection of two roads of equal importance, where there is no such sign, vehicles coming from the right have priority. However, emergency vehicles, with a blue light or siren, and trams and buses have absolute priority at any intersection and, indeed, on any road. Buses also have right of way when leaving bus stops after the driver has signalled his intention to pull out.

Road signs

utca: street
ter: square
korut: boulevard

Seat belts

If fitted, compulsory use in front and rear seats.

Signalling

The use of horns in built-up areas is not permitted, except in case of danger. It is permitted outside built-up areas, when necessary.

Speed limits

Built-up areas: motorcycles, cars with or without caravan/trailer 31mph (50kmh). Outside built-up areas: motorcycles, cars 50mph (80kmh), dual carriageways 62mph (100kmh), motorways 75mph (120kmh). Car with caravan/trailer on normal roads and dual carriageways 44mph (70kmh), on motorways 50mph (80kmh).

Tolls

See page 77.

Traffic offences

On-the-spot fines up to 2000 HUF are imposed and collected by the police. Credit cards are not accepted. Alternatively, fines may be paid by post within 15 days.

General information

Banks

Open Mon-Thurs 0800-1500, Fri 0800-1300.

Currency

Forint. The official abbreviation of the forint is HUF, but the old abbreviation Ft. is still used. Visitors must be in possession of the equivalent of 5,000 HUF in hard currency. Exemptions from this regulation are visitors holding a credit card, letter of invitation or accommodation vouchers issued by a travel agency.

Museums

Open Tue-Sat 1000-1800.

Public holidays

New Year; 15 Mar; Easter Monday; Whitsun; Labour Day; Constitution Day, 20 Aug; Proclamation of the Republic, 23 Oct; Christmas, 25, 26 Dec.

Shops

Open Mon-Fri 1000-1800, Sat 0900-1300.

Visa

British Nationals do not require a visa for stays less than 180 days.

Tourist office

Hungarian National Tourist Office, 46 Eaton Place, London SW1X 8AL. Tel: 0171 823 1032. Official website: www.hungarytourism.hu

Republic of Ireland

Motoring information

Accidents and emergencies

Police, Fire, Ambulance Tel: 999 and 112.

Carriage of children

Not permitted under 12 in front seat, unless the seat is equipped with a child restraint.

Drinking and driving

A person convicted of driving or attempting to drive with a blood alcohol level exceeding 80mg will be liable to a severe penalty.

Fuel

Petrol stations are usually open from 0730 to 2200, and some are open 24 hours. Leaded petrol: Super (98 octane) available. Unleaded petrol: widely available. Diesel: widely available. Credit cards: accepted. Spare fuel: although up to 10 litres may be imported duty free in containers, do remember that it is illegal to carry spare fuel on ferries.

Internal ferries

A car ferry operates across the River Shannon from Tarbert (Co. Kerry) to Killimer (Co. Clare). The ferry leaves Killimer hourly on the hour, and Tarbert hourly on the half-hour. Crossing time is 30 minutes.
A 10-minute car ferry service operates between

Ballyhack (Co. Wexford) and Passage East (Co. Waterford). First sailing 0720 weekdays, 0930 Sunday. Last sailing 2200 in summer, 2000 in winter.

Lighting

Foglights may only be used in fog or falling snow.

Parking

The usual restrictions apply as in Great Britain. Parking meters operate from Monday to Saturday from 0800 to 1830 and the maximum authorised parking time is 2 hours. Free use of unexpired time on meters is authorised. On-the-spot fines may be levied for parking offences.

Road signs

The 'Give Way' sign is a red triangle with the point downwards, and words *Yield Right of Way* or *Geill sli.*

Signalling

Horns must not be used between 2330 and 0700 on any road where a permanent speed limit is in force.

Speed limits

Built-up areas: 30mph (48kmh); outside built-up areas: 60mph (96kmh); motorways: 70mph (112kmh).
On certain roads, and clearly marked, the speed limits are 40mph (64kmh) or 50mph (80kmh). Cars towing a trailer/caravan are limited to 50mph (80kmh) on all roads.

Temporary importation of vehicles

Drivers of motor caravans, caravans and trailers will be issued with a temporary importation permit by Irish Customs at their port of arrival.
A temporarily imported vehicle must not be driven by an Irish resident.

Tolls

A toll of 80p is charged for cars on the Dublin Ring Road (M50).

Traffic offences

If a motorist has committed an offence the Garda Siochana (Civic Guard) may issue the person with a notice instructing the offender to pay a fine within 21 days at a Garda Station. The offender has an alternative choice of letting the case go to court.

General information

Banks

Open Mon–Fri 1000–1230 and 1330–1500 (in Dublin, until 1700 on Thursdays).

Currency

Irish punt.

Museums

Generally open 1000–1700 daily except public holidays.

Passport

British citizens born in the United Kingdom do not require a passport to visit Ireland.

Public holidays

New Year's Day; St Patrick's Day, 17 Mar; Easter; first Mon in June and Aug; last Mon in Oct; Christmas.

Shops

Open Mon–Sat 0900–1730/1800.

Tourist office

Irish Tourist Board, 150 New Bond Street, London W1Y 0AQ, Tel: 0171-493 3201
Official website: www.ireland.travel.ie

Italy

Motoring information

National motoring organisation

Automobile Club d'Italia (ACI), FIA, Via Marsala 8, 00185 Roma. Tel: (06) 49981. Office hours: Mon–Sat 0800–1400 and 1500–1900. Offices in most large towns.

Accidents and emergencies

Police Tel: 112, Fire Brigade Tel: 115, Ambulance Tel: 118.

Breakdowns

In the case of breakdown, Tel: 116. This puts the traveller in touch with the ACI breakdown service. Motoring visitors can also use this number for urgent medical or legal advice.

Carriage of children

Children aged between 4 and 12 must occupy a front or rear seat which is equipped with a special restraint.

Car theft

To combat the major problem of car theft, the authorities are increasing the number of spot checks of foreign registered vehicles.
Drivers must be able to present vehicle documents, including authorisation from the vehicle owner to use the vehicle, and personal papers. Failure to do so can result in confiscation of the vehicle.

Drinking and driving

The blood alcohol legal limit is 80mg.

Fuel

On motorways, petrol stations are open 24 hours. On other roads, fuel is available (May to September) 0700–1230, and 1530–1930. From October to April, petrol stations close at 1900. Only 25% of petrol stations on these roads are open on Sundays and public holidays, and are subsequently closed on Mondays. Opening hours are displayed, along with the address of the nearest garage open.
Fuel prices are increased by 20 lire on motorways with a further 20 lire surcharge for night service (not applicable at automatic pumps).
Leaded petrol: Super (98/100 octane) available.
Unleaded petrol: Super (95 octane) available; pump legend benzina sensa piombo.
Diesel: available; pump legend gasolio.
Credit cards: accepted at motorway service stations and at 70% of petrol stations on ordinary roads.
Spare fuel: it is prohibited to import and carry fuel in cans. Coupons: the coupon scheme has been discontinued.

Lighting

It is compulsory to use vehicle lights half an hour after sunset until half an hour before sunrise. Main beam headlights can only be used outside towns, and when no other vehicle is approaching. At all other times, only low beam headlights can be used.
Lights must be used under bridges and dipped lights must be used in tunnels.
Foglights should only be used in bad visibility.

Orange Badge holders

Local authorities are responsible for parking concessions. Generally public transport has priority in town centres and private cars may sometimes be banned. However, the authorities must take special measures to let badge holders take their vehicles into social, cultural and recreational activity areas.
Reserved parking bays are provided, indicated by signs with the international symbol.

Overhanging load

An overhanging load (e.g. bicycle carried behind car or caravan) must be indicated by a square panel 50cm by 50cm with reflectorised red and white diagonal stripes.
The sign is available from motor caravan/caravan dealerships in the UK. A fine of 100,000 lire may be imposed if the sign is not displayed

Overtaking

You may overtake on the right when the other driver has signalled he is turning left and has moved to the centre of the road, or when travel is in parallel lanes.

Parking

This is allowed on the right side of the road, except on motorways (autostrada) and in places where you would not park in Britain.
There are Blue Zones in all major towns, indicated by road signs. Within these zones a parking disc must be displayed from Monday to Saturday (except holidays) 0900–1430 and 1600–2000. The maximum period is one hour. Discs are obtained from the tourist and automobile organisations and petrol stations.
There are also Green Zones where parking is strictly prohibited on weekdays 0800–0930 and 1430–1600.

In Vénezia: Owing to the limited parking facilities at the Venezia end of the causeway, especially in the Piazzale Roma, it is advisable to park at one of the special car parks on the mainland. The car parks are linked by ferry and bus services to destinations in Venezia.
In Roma: Parking is strictly prohibited in the central area on weekdays, indicated by a sign reading *zona tutelato*. Illegal parking will result in a fine and a prison sentence.
In Firenze (Florence): Vehicles are banned from the centre on weekdays 0730–1830. Visitors staying within the area may stop to offload luggage, but then must park outside the restricted area.

Priority

On three-lane roads, the middle lane is reserved for overtaking. At crossroads, give way to traffic from the right. Outside built-up areas priority must be given to vehicles travelling on national roads (*strade stratali*).
On certain mountain roads, a red circular sign bearing a black post horn on a white triangle indicates that vehicles are required to stop at the approach of buses belonging to the postal services.

Road signs

Most conform to the international pattern. Other road signs which may be encountered are:
Entrata: entrance
Incrocio: crossroads
Lavori in corso: roadworks ahead
Passaggio a livello: level crossing
Rallentare: slow down
Senso Vietato: no entry
Sosta Autorizzata: parking permitted (followed by indication of times)
Sosta Vietata: no parking
Svolta: bend
Uscita: exit
Vietato Ingresso Veicoli: no entry for vehicles
Vietato Transito Autocarri: closed to heavy vehicles

Signalling

In built-up areas use of the horn is prohibited except in cases of immediate danger. At night, flashing headlights may be used instead of a horn.

Outside built-up areas, when it is required that warning of approach be given, the use of the horn is compulsory.

Speed limits

Built-up areas: all vehicles 31mph (50kmh); outside built-up areas: motorcycles over 150cc and cars on secondary roads 55mph (90kmh), main roads 68mph (110kmh); motorways: 80mph (130kmh).
Motorcaravans between 3.5 and 12 tonnes: outside built up areas 50mph (80kmh), motorways 62mph (100kmh).
Motorcaravans over 12 tonnes and car towing a caravan or trailer are limited to 44mph (70kmh) *outside* built up areas and 50mph (80kmh) on motorways.

Tolls

Tolls are payable on the *autostrada* network (see page 77). Credit cards are accepted for payment on the A4, A22, A28 and A32 motorways only. On most motorways (except Sicily) motorists may pay for tolls with a magnetic card called a VIACARD. The card is available in varying denominations from toll booths, service areas, certain banks and tourist offices. The card is valid until expiry of credit and can be used on subsequent visits.

Traffic offences

The police can impose a fine on the driver of a foreign registered vehicle and collect one quarter of the maximum fine on the spot.
If the driver wishes to contest the fine or refuses to pay, a guarantee for half the maximum amount must be deposited, either in cash (foreign currency accepted) or in the form of a surety. If the guarantee is not deposited, the driving licence may be withdrawn.
If the licence is not available, the car may be confiscated until the fine is paid.

General information

Banks

Open Mon–Fri 0830–1330 and 1500–1600.

Currency

Lire.

Public holidays

New Year's Day; Easter Monday; Liberation Day, 25 Apr; Labour Day; Assumption, 15 Aug; All Saints Day, 1 Nov; Immaculate Conception, 8 Dec; Christmas, 25, 26 Dec
It is wise to check locally for shop and bank closing times on special Feast days.

Purchase of meals and goods

Visitors to Italy should obtain a specially numbered receipt (*Ricevuta fiscale*) when paying for a meal in restaurants, hotels, etc and when purchasing goods.
This fiscal receipt must show the amount you have paid for each part of the meal and the VAT you paid. Visitors must ensure that this receipt is issued, as a fine may be imposed for non-compliance.

Shops

Open Mon–Sat 0830/0900–1300 and 1530/1600–1930/2000 with some variations in the north, where the lunch break is shorter and shops close earlier.

Tourist office

Italian State Tourist Office, 1 Princes Street, London W1R 8AY, Tel: 0891-600280 (calls cost 60p per minute at all times).

Luxembourg

Motoring information

National motoring organisation

Automobile Club du Grand Duché de Luxembourg (ACL), FIA, 13 route de Longwy, 8007, Bertrange. Tel: 450045-1. Office hours: Mon–Fri 0830–1200 and 1330–1800.

Accidents and emergencies

Police Tel: 113, Fire Brigade and Ambulance Tel: 112.

Carriage of children

A child under 12, or less than 1.5 metres in height, may only occupy a front seat in a special safety-approved seat. In the rear, a child should be seated in a child seat, or use a seat belt.

Drinking and driving

The blood alcohol legal limit is 80mg.

Fuel

Leaded petrol: Super (98 octane) available.
Unleaded petrol: Super (95 octane) available; pump legend *essence sans plomb*.
Diesel: available.
Credit cards: Visa and Eurocard accepted.
Spare fuel: it is prohibited to purchase and carry spare fuel in cans.

Lighting

Use dipped headlights when visibility is reduced due to fog, heavy rain or snow during daylight hours. It is compulsory to use dipped headlights in built-up areas. In other places vehicles must have dipped or undipped headlights. Motorcyclists must use dipped headlights day and night.

Orange Badge holders

In most urban areas reserved parking spaces are provided and indicated by round blue and red no waiting or rectangular white and blue parking signs with the international symbol.
Badge holders are generally not allowed to exceed the parking time limit.

Overtaking

Avoid when this might endanger or obstruct traffic.

Parking

A Blue Zone parking area exists in Luxembourg City, Esch-sur-Alzette, Dudelange and Wiltz. Parking discs follow the usual pattern and are obtainable from the ACL, police stations, local tourist office, shops, etc. Luxembourg City has coin parking meters and ticket parking – tickets obtainable at dispensing boxes. Illegally parked vehicles will be clamped by the police.

Priority

The rule of the road is keep to the right, overtake on the left. At a crossing of two roads in the same category, traffic from the right has priority. In towns, give priority to traffic coming from the right, unless the crossing is marked with a triangular sign.

Signalling

Unnecessary use of the horn is prohibited. Do not use it between nightfall and dawn, or in built-up areas, except in an emergency.
During the day, warning of approach should be given before overtaking another vehicle, or where visibility is restricted or whenever road safety requires it. At night, in these circumstances, it is compulsory to flash headlights.

Speed limits

Built-up areas: 31mph (50kmh); outside built-up areas: 56mph (90kmh); motorways: 74mph (120kmh).
Cars towing a caravan or trailer are limited to 46mph (75kmh); outside built-up areas, and 56mph (90kmh) on motorways.

Traffic offences

On-the-spot fines are imposed by police in cases of traffic offences.

General information

Banks

Open Mon–Fri 0830–1200 and 1330–1630.

Currency

Luxembourg and Belgian francs.

Public holidays

New Year's Day; Carnival Day mid February*; Easter Monday; May Day; Ascension; Whit Monday; National Day, 23 June; Assumption, 15 Aug; All Saints; All Souls*; Christmas, 25, 26 Dec. (*although not an official holiday, banks and offices are closed and most shops are closed, particularly in the afternoon.)

Shops

Open Mon 1400–1830, Tue–Sat 0830–1200 and 1400–1830.

Tourist office

Luxembourg Tourist Office, 122 Regent Street, London W1R 5FE, Tel: 0171-434 2800
Official website: www.luxembourg.co.uk

Netherlands

Motoring information

National motoring organisation

Koninklijke Nederlandsche Automobiel Club (KNAC), FIA, Wassenaarseweg 220, 25916 EC Den Haag. Tel: (070) 383 1612. Office hours: Mon–Fri 0830–1700.

Accidents and emergencies

Police, Fire Brigade and Ambulance, Tel: 112

Carriage of children

Children under three must travel in the rear with a safety system adapted to their size.
Those aged three to 12 may travel in a front seat if in a special safety seat.

Drinking and driving

The blood alcohol legal limit is 50mg.

Fuel

Leaded petrol: Super (98 octane) available (contains lead substitute).
Unleaded petrol: Super (95 and 98 octane) available; pump legend *loodvrije benzine*.
Diesel: available.
Credit cards: accepted.
Spare fuel: 10 litres of petrol in a can may be imported duty free.

Internal ferries

A car ferry service operates across the Westerschelde estuary between Breskens and Vlissingen, and further east between Perkpolder and Kruiningen. Journey time is 20 mins and 15 mins respectively.

Lighting

Parked vehicles do not have to be illuminated at

night, provided they are parked in a built-up area, within 30 metres of a street lighting point, or in an official car park. Inside built-up areas only dipped headlights (low beam) are permitted. Dipped or full headlights must be used in fog.

Orange Badge holders

Badge holders may park as follows:
- in reserved parking places for people with disabilities
- for an unlimited time in a parking disc zone, without a parking disc
- outside parking bays in a residential area with pedestrian priority for up to 3 hours using a parking disc
- in parking spaces where a parking ban applies, for up to 3 hours using a parking disc
- on a broken yellow line for up to 3 hours using a parking disc

Badge holders should, however, be aware that the Netherlands has its own system of signs and they should enquire locally if in doubt.

Overtaking

Do not cross a continuous white line on the road, even to make a left turn.
You may overtake stationary trams on the right at moderate speed, provided no inconvenience is caused to persons entering or leaving the tram. The overtaking of moving trams is normally permitted only on the right, although if there is insufficient room and no danger to oncoming traffic, vehicles may overtake on the left. The 'overtaking prohibited' sign does not apply to scooters or solo motorcycles. Do follow correct lanes, these are well marked with arrows.

Parking

Do not park on roads signposted 'No Parking', in front of driveways or where you may obscure road, street or traffic signs; on priority roads outside built-up areas.
Do not halt a vehicle on roads signposted *Stop-verbod* – a blue disc with a red border and red diagonals; on access roads to and from main highways; cycling paths or footpaths, or along a yellow line or black and white line painted on road or pavement alongside a bus stop; in the middle of a three-lane road, or on a road with more than three lanes (this does not stop passengers getting in or out of a car); on level crossings.

Blue Zones have been introduced in most towns and free parking discs can be obtained from police stations.
A parking fee is charged at guarded car parks. There are also parking meters. Wheel clamps will be used on illegally parked vehicles.

Priority

Priority roads are indicated by diamond-shaped yellow signs with white borders.
At junctions where the sign 'major road ahead' or 'stop, major road ahead' is displayed, priority must be given to all traffic on that road.
At the intersection of two roads of the same class where there are no signs, traffic from the right has preference.
Motor vehicles have right of way over slow traffic, such as bicycles.
Ambulances, fire engines, police cars and emergency rescue vehicles always have right of way.
Trams have priority at intersections of equal importance but they must yield right of way to traffic on priority roads.
At intersections, cyclists proceeding straight ahead have priority over all traffic. At pedestrian crossings do give a pedestrian absolute priority if he is on the zebra crossing first.

Road signs

Most conform to the international pattern but other road signs which may be seen are:
>*Doorgaand verkeer gestremd*: no throughway
>*Langzaam rijden*: slow down
>*Opspattend Grind*: loose grit
>*Pas op: filevorming*: attention: single or double lane traffic ahead
>*Rechtsaf toegeslaan*: right turn allowed
>*Tegenliggers*: traffic from the opposite direction
>*Wegomlegging*: detour
>*Werk in uitvoering*: road building in progress

A blue sign with a white house emblem – *Woonerf*: built-up area – can mean:
(1) drive at walking pace (children playing in street);
(2) pedestrians have right of way;
(3) bicycles from the right have priority;
(4) park only in zones marked 'P'.

Seat belts

If fitted, compulsory use in front seats.

Signalling

Sound your horn where there is any risk to other road users.
At night you should give warning by flashing headlights instead, unless this might cause interference to other traffic, in which case the horn may be used.

Speed limits

Built-up areas: 31mph (50kmh); outside built-up areas: 50-62mph (80-100kmh), cars towing a caravan or trailer with one axle, 50mph (80kmh); motorways: 74mph (120kmh) and minimum speed 37mph (60kmh).

Traffic offences

In some districts, on-the-spot fines are imposed and collected by the police.

General information

Banks

Open Mon–Fri 0900–1600. At border towns, exchange offices (GWK) are open Mon–Sat, also often Sun and in the evenings.

Bicycles

Visitors should be prepared for heavy cycle traffic, particularly at peak hours.
Cycle lanes marked by continuous white lines are prohibited to vehicles.
Cycle lanes marked by a broken white line may be used by motor vehicles if they do not obstruct cyclists.

Currency

Guilder (florin).

Museums

Open Tue–Fri 1000–1700, Sat and Sun 1100–1700, or 1300–1700.

Public holidays

New Year's Day; Good Friday; Easter Monday; Queen's Birthday, 30 Apr; Liberation Day, 5 May; Ascension; Whit Monday; Christmas, 25, 26 Dec.

Shops

Department stores open Mon–Fri 0830/0900–1730/1800, Sat 0830/0900–1600/1700. Food shops open Mon–Sat 0800–1800.
Traders required by law to close their shops for one half day per week.
Local regulations say when all shops will be closed either until 1300, or from 1300 onwards.

Tourist office

Netherlands Board of Tourism, 18 Buckingham Gate, London SW1E 6LB, Tel: 0891-717777 (calls cost 60p per minute at all times), postal address PO Box 523, London SW1E 6NT
Official website: www.visitholland.com

Norway

Motoring information

National motoring organisation

Kongelig Norsk Automobilklub (KNA), FIA, Drammensveien 20-C, 0255 Oslo. Tel: (47) 22-56 19 00. Office hours: Mon–Fri 0830–1600 (1500 in summer).

Accidents and emergencies

Police Tel: 112, Fire Brigade Tel: 110, Ambulance Tel: 113.
After an accident it is compulsory to exchange name, address and name of insurance company.

Breakdowns

During the summer season road patrols are maintained on most mountain passes and on certain main roads.

Carriage of children

Children under 4 years of age must be in a special restraint system. Children over 4 years of age must use a child restraint or a seat belt.

Drinking and driving

The blood alcohol legal limit is 50mg.

Fuel

Petrol stations are generally open between 0700 and 2200 hours. Some petrol stations remain open 24 hours a day in cities.
Leaded petrol: Super (98 octane) available.
Unleaded petrol: Super (95 octane) available; pump legend *blyfritt kraftstoff*.
Diesel: available.
Credit cards: major cards accepted at larger petrol stations.
Spare fuel: no more than 15 litres are recommended to carry in approved storage cans, which may be imported duty free.

Internal car ferries

Full details of car ferry services within Norway are given in a special timetable, available from the Norwegian Tourist Board annually in March on receipt of a large SAE with 50 pence postage.

Lighting

It is compulsory to use dipped headlights at all times.
Foglights are not compulsory, but if used must be in conjunction with other lights. They may be used in fog or falling snow and in clear weather on winding roads.

Mountain passes

Many of the high mountain roads are closed during the winter, duration of closure depending on weather conditions.
However, some mountain passes are kept open all year, eg Road No. 11 (Oslo–Bergen/Stavanger) across Haukelifjell mountain, the E6 (Oslo–Trondheim) across Dovrefjell mountain, and Road No. 7 (Oslo–Bergen) over the Hardangervidda plateau.

Orange Badge holders

There are no formal reciprocal arrangements with Norway, but it is understood badge holders are allowed to park in meter or paying parking spaces free of charge and without time limit. They may also use spaces marked with signs indicating reserved parking for disabled persons

entitled to parking concessions, but these may be limited.

Overtaking

In Oslo, overtake trams on the right (you can overtake them on the left if in motion in a one-way street or if there is no room on the right).

Parking

Do not park on main roads; where visibility is restricted; where there is a sign *All Stans Forbudt* (No stopping allowed), or you may have your car towed away.
Parking regulations in Norwegian towns are very strict, and parking offences are invariably subject to fines. Parking meters are in use in the main towns.
Free use of unexpired time on meters is authorised.
There are three types of parking meter: Yellow – 1 hour parking, Grey – 2 hours, and Brown – 3 hours.

Priority

Give way to traffic from the right, except on some main roads which are given permanent priority. Intersecting junctions will bear the international priority symbol.
Vehicles climbing uphill must be given priority, and down-hill drivers must reverse into a parking bay if necessary. Traffic on roundabouts has priority.
Trams always have right of way.

Road signs

Arbeide pa Vegen: roadworks ahead
Bakketopp: hill top
Enveiskjøring: one-way traffic
Ferist: cattle grid
Gammel Veg: old road
Grøfterens: ditching work
Ikke Møte: no passing, single line traffic
Kjør Sakte: drive slowly
Løs Grus: loose gravel
Møteplass: passing bay
Omkjøring: diversion
Rasteplass: lay-by
Svake Kanter: soft verges
Veg under Anlegg: road under construction
Veiarbeide: roadworks

Signalling

Use horns, traffic indicators and lights only when necessary to avoid accidents.

Speed limits

Built-up areas: 31mph (50kmh); outside built-up areas and on motorways: 50–56mph (80–90kmh). Outside built-up areas, cars towing a caravan or trailer (with brakes) 50mph (80kmh); (without brakes) 37mph (60kmh).

Tolls

All vehicles entering Bergen by road on a weekday must pay a toll of 5 Kr. No charge at weekends or on public holidays.
Cars or vehicles up to 3.5 tonnes entering Oslo pay a toll of 12 Kr and a toll of 11 Kr to enter Trondheim.

Traffic offences

Police are empowered to impose and collect fines on the spot in cases of traffic offences.

General information

Banks

Open Mon–Fri 0815–1500 (1530 in winter). Some banks open until 1700 on Thursdays.

Currency

Krone (plural kroner).

Public holidays

New Year's Day; Maundy Thurs; Good Friday; Easter Monday; Labour Day; Constitution Day, 17 May; Whit Monday; Ascension Day; Christmas, 25 and 26 Dec.

Shops

Open Mon/Tues/Wed/Fri 0900–1700, Thu 0900–1800, Sat 0900–1300. In July some close at 1500.

Tourist office

Norwegian National Tourist Office, Charles House, 5–11 Lower Regent Street, London SW1Y 4LR, Tel: 0171-839 6255
Official website: www.tourist.no

Poland

Motoring information

National motoring organisation

Polski Zwiazek Motorowy (PZM), FIA, 66 Kazimierzowska Street, PL-02-518 Warszawa. Tel: (48) 22 499 361, 22 499 212. Touring office: Autotour s.r.l., 85 Solec Street, 00-950 Warszawa. Tel: (48) 22 498 449. Head Office hours: Mon-Fri 0745-1545; PZM Touring office hours: Mon-Fri 0800-1600.
Auto Assistance, 19 Sandomierska Street, 00-950 Warszawa. Tel: (48) 22-290 374.

Accidents and emergencies

Police Tel: 997, Fire Brigade Tel: 998, Ambulance Tel: 999.
If you are involved in an accident you must report it to the nearest police station and Insurance Association. It is an offence not to render first aid to accident victims or to leave the scene of an accident.

Breakdowns

The Polski Zwiazek Motorway operates a road patrol service within a 25km radius of towns with a PZM office. Details are obtained from PZM frontier offices and provincial touring offices. In most towns, for breakdown assistance Tel: 981. Technical help is free to motorists belonging to FIA Clubs for repairs within the 25km area, which can be effected within an hour. For serious breakdowns the vehicle will be towed to a garage.

Carriage of children

Children under 10 are not allowed to travel on the front seat unless the vehicle has a child restraint seat.

Crash helmets

Compulsory for motorcyclists and passengers.

Drinking and driving

The blood alcohol legal limit is 20mg.

Fuel

Petrol stations generally open 0800-1900. In large

towns, some stations open 24 hours.
Leaded petrol: Regular (86 octane) and Super
(94/98 octane) available.
Unleaded petrol: Regular (82.5 octane) and Super
(91 octane) available; pump legend *benzyna
bezolowiu*.
Diesel: available.
Spare fuel: up to 10 litres of fuel may be imported
and exported.

Lighting

At night in built-up areas, where street lighting is
insufficient, drivers must use dipped headlights.
During bad visibility, drivers must use passing
lights and/or foglights. Use of front foglights is
permitted on winding roads at night. Motorcyclists
must use headlights at all times outside built-up
areas. Between 1 November and 1 March, it is
compulsory for all vehicles to use dipped
headlights at all times.

Orange Badge holders

Badge holders are entitled to special parking
concessions. They can park in areas where
parking is normally for a restricted time or
prohibited, provided the disabled permit is
displayed behind the windscreen.

Overtaking

The usual restrictions apply. Trams may be
overtaken on the right. At tram stops without
pedestrian islands, motorists should stop to let
passengers walk between tram and pavement.
During bad visibility drivers must give short
audible warning signals before overtaking.

Parking

Parking is prohibited on certain streets signposted
to that effect. On unlit streets, parking lights are
obligatory during the hours of darkness.

Priority

In general, priority is given to vehicles coming
from the right, but vehicles on major roads and
roundabouts have right of way. Overtake trams on
the right.

Road signs

International road signs.

Seat belts

If fitted, compulsory use in front and rear seats.

Signalling

Do not sound your horn in built-up areas. Some
localities display signs prohibiting the use of horns
in particular areas. Warning of approach should be
given by flashing headlights and by short horn
signals when driving in fog.

Speed limits

Built-up areas: 37mph (60kmh); outside built-up
areas: 56mph (90kmh); motorways: 68mph
(110kmh). The minimum speed on motorways is
24mph (40kmh). Cars towing a caravan or trailer,
44mph (70kmh) outside built-up areas, including
motorways.
In addition to built-up areas there are residential
zones, indicated by 'entry/exit' signs, where the
maximum speed permitted is 12mph (20kmh).

Traffic offences

Motorists who infringe traffic regulations may
receive a verbal or written warning, or an on-the-
spot fine of between 50 & 500 zlotys. A receipt
must be provided by the police officer.

General information

Banks

Usually open Mon-Fri 0800-1700/1900,
Sat (variable) 0800-1300.

Currency

Zloty. Currency control regulations have been
lifted and as a result the compulsory daily
exchange procedure has been abolished, as have
accommodation vouchers. Foreign currency can
be exchanged at frontier posts; branches of the
Narodowy Bank Polski; the Bank of Commerce in
Warszawa; hotel exchange offices, travel agencies
and PZM frontier offices. It is essential to keep the
conversion slips issued when currency is
exchanged.

Public holidays

New Year's Day; Easter Monday; Labour Day;
Constitution Day, 3 May; Corpus Christi; Feast of

the Assumption, 15 Aug; All Saints, 1 Nov; Independence Day, 11 Nov; Christmas, 25, 26 Dec.

Shops

Food shops open Mon-Fri 0600-1900, Sat 0700-1300. Other shops open Mon-Fri 1100-2000, Sat 0900-1600.

Visa

No longer required by British nationals.

Tourist office

Polish National Tourist Office, Remo House, 310-312 Regent Street, London W1R 5AJ. Tel: 0171 580 6688.

Portugal

Motoring information

National motoring organisation

Automóvel Club de Portugal (ACP), FIA, Rua Rosa Araújo 24, 1200 Lisboa. Tel: 1-356 39 31. Office hours: Mon–Fri 0900–1300 and 1400–1645. Touring reception: (Apr–Sep) Mon–Fri 0900–1730; (Oct–Mar) 0900–1645.

Accidents and emergencies

Police, Fire Brigade and Ambulance Tel: 112.

Breakdowns

For ACP breakdown service south of Pombal, Tel: Lisboa 942 50 95 and to the north, Tel: Porto 830 11 27.

Carriage of children

Not permitted under the age of 12 in the front seat, unless a child safety seat is fitted.

Drinking and driving

The blood alcohol legal limit is 50mg.

Fuel

Petrol stations are open 0700–2200, 0700–2400, or 24 hours.
Leaded petrol: Super (98 octane) available.
Unleaded petrol: Super (95/98 octane) available; pump legend *gasolina sin plomo*.
Diesel: available; pump legend *o gasóleo*.
Credit cards: accepted. Purchase of fuel with a credit card incurs a surcharge of 100 Esc.
Spare fuel: it is permitted to carry spare fuel.

Internal ferries

A car ferry service, operated by the Transado company, crosses the Sado estuary between Setúbal and Troia.
There are 10 crossings per day between midnight and 2300, journey time 15 minutes. Services also operate from Lisboa across the Tagus (Tejo) estuary to Cacilhas, Barreiro, Montijo and Porto Brandão.

Lighting

In built-up areas, use dipped headlights at night. Motorcyclists should use lights at all times.

Orange Badge holders

Parking places indicated by signs with the international symbol are reserved for badge holders. They cannot park where it is prohibited by a general regulation or specific sign.

Overtaking

The overtaking of stationary trams is permitted only if there is an island for embarking or disembarking passengers.

Parking

Parked vehicles must face in the same direction as moving traffic, except where parking is officially allowed on one side of the road only. Parking meters are in use in Lisbon, Oporto, Setúbal, etc. Illegally parked vehicles will be immobilised and released only upon payment of a fine.

Priority

Do allow priority to traffic coming from the right.

Registration document

A special certificate, Autorizacao, will be required if the vehicle is not registered in your name – available from RAC Travel Information, Tel: 0891 347 333 (calls charged at 60p per minute at all times).

Roads

Roads are classified as follows: motorways (AE), principal roads (IP), national roads (EN), municipal roads (EM), other municipal roads (CM).

Signalling

Do not use the horn except to signal danger. Use flashing headlights at night and hand or mechanical indicators during the day.

Speed limits

Built-up areas: 31mph (50kmh); outside built-up areas: 56/62mph (90/100kmh); motorways: 74mph (120kmh).
Cars towing a caravan or trailer are limited to 31mph (50kmh) in built-up areas, 43/50mph (70/80kmh) outside built-up areas, and 62mph (100kmh) on motorways. Minimum speed on motorways is 24mph (40kmh) unless otherwise indicated. On the 25 de Abril Bridge, Lisboa, maintain a speed of 18–31mph (30–50kmh). Visiting motorists who have held a full licence for under a year are limited to 56mph (90kmh), and a yellow disc (from ACP border offices) showing the figure '90' must be displayed.

Temporary importation of caravans

It is recommended to obtain a temporary importation form from a frontier customs office (*Delegaçao Aduaneirá*).
This can be requested by police for foreign registered vehicles.
An inventory of the contents of a caravan must be provided on plain paper or by filling in a form available at the frontier.

Tolls

Payable on certain roads (see page 79).

Traffic offences

The police are authorised to impose on-the-spot fines. A receipt is issued to show that the fine has been paid.

Fines are imposed for unauthorised parking, speeding, excess blood alcohol level, and failure to wear seat belts, if fitted.
A motorist who refuses to pay the fine must pay a deposit to cover the maximum fine for the offence committed.
If the deposit is not paid, the police will confiscate the vehicle.

General information

Banks

Open Mon–Fri 0830–1445. Some large city banks operate a currency exchange service 1830–2300.

Currency

Escudos.

Museums

Open Tue–Sun 1000–1230 and 1400–1700.

Public holidays

New Year's Day; Carnival (Shrove Tuesday); Good Friday; Liberty Day, 25 Apr; Labour Day; Corpus Christi; Portugal Day, 10 June; St António, 13 June (Lisboa); São João, 24 June (Porto); Assumption, 15 Aug; Republic Day, 5 Oct; All Saints, 1 Nov; Independence Day, 1 Dec; Immaculate Conception, 8 Dec; Christmas, 24, 25 or 25, 26 Dec.

Shops

Open Mon–Fri 0900–1300 and 1500–1900, Sat 0900–1300. Shopping centres are open every day from 1000–2400.

Tourist office

Portuguese National Tourist Office, 22–25a Sackville Street, London W1X 2LY, Tel: 0171-494 1441
Official website: www.portugal.org/tourism

Visitor Identification

All visitors should ensure identity documents, e.g. passports are carried at all times when driving. Failure to do so will result in an on-the-spot fine.

Romania

Motoring information

National motoring organisation

Automobil Clubul Român (ACR), FIA , Str. Tache Ionescu 27, 70154 Bucuresti 22. Tel: 1-850 2595. Office hours: Mon-Fri 0800-1600.

Accidents and emergencies

Police Tel: 955, Fire Brigade Tel: 981, Ambulance, Tel: 961. All accidents must be reported to the police. If the vehicle is damaged, a report must be obtained from the police to facilitate export of the vehicle from the country. A visitor in possession of a valid insurance policy will receive all assistance from CAROM (State Insurance Administration).

Breakdowns

For breakdown assistance please refer to European Motoring Assistance documentation.

Carriage of children

Children under 12 are not allowed to travel on the front seat.

Crash helmets

Compulsory for motorcyclists and passengers.

Drinking and driving

Do not drink and drive: blood alcohol legal limit is 0mg.

Fuel

Leaded petrol: Super (96/98 octane) available. Unleaded petrol: Super (98 octane) widely available; pump legend *benzina fara plumb*. Diesel: available.
Spare fuel: up to 10 litres of fuel in cans may be imported duty free. Export of fuel: A tax is levied on all petrol and diesel exported from Romania. Coupons: no longer required.

Lighting

In built-up areas, where roads are not lit, undipped headlights may be used for passing and at intersections. Where roads are lit, drivers must use dipped headlights only.

Overtaking

All vehicles must be overtaken on the left, except for trams which are overtaken on the right.

Parking

Stop or park vehicles on the right-hand side of the road in the direction of the traffic. Parking is prohibited on the carriageway of national highways.

Priority

At roundabouts, priority must be given to vehicles coming from the right. Vehicles already in the roundabout traffic must give way to vehicles entering the roundabout, as the latter come from the right.

Seat belts

Recommended.

Signalling

Use of the horn is prohibited in towns 2200-0600. At night, warning must be given by the use of lights. In Bucuresti and other towns, use of the horn is prohibited, and signs to this effect – *claxonarea interzisa* – warn motorists of this regulation.

Speed limits

Cars with or without caravan/trailer: built-up areas 37mph (60kmh); outside built-up areas and on motorways: under 1000cc, 44mph (70kmh), 1100-1800cc, 50mph (80kmh), over 1800cc 56mph (90kmh). Motorcycles: built-up areas 25mph (40kmh), outside built-up areas 37mph (60kmh).

Tolls

Charged for crossing the River Danube from Giurgiu to Ruse (Bulgaria), and from Giurgeni to Vadu Oii.

Traffic offences

Members of the Militia (police) may impose fines on the spot for violation of traffic regulations.

General information

Banks

Open Mon-Fri 0900-1200, 1300-1500, Sat 0900-1230.

Currency

Leu (plural lei).

Public holidays

New Year, 1, 2 Jan; International Labour Day, 1, 2 May; National Holiday, 23 24 Aug.

Shops

Open Mon-Fri 0800-2000, Sat 0800-2100. Sun 0800-1200.

Visa

British nationals must hold a valid passport and visa, available from: Romanian Consulate, 8 Palace Green, London W8, Tel: 0171-937 9667; or at the border and airports.

Tourist office

Romanian Tourist Promotion Office, 83a Marylebone High Street, London W1M 3DE. Tel: 0171 224 3692.

Slovakia

Motoring information

National motoring organisation

Ustredni Automotoklub SR, FIA, Wolkrova ul.c.4, 851 01 Bratislava. Tel: 7-85 09 11. Office hours Mon-Fri 0745-1645.

Accidents and emergencies

Police Tel: 158, Fire Brigade Tel: 150, Ambulance Tel: 155.
If an accident causes bodily injury or material damage exceeding 1,000 SK, it must be reported to the police immediately. A certificate will be issued by the police to facilitate export of the vehicle. Accidents involving locally registered vehicles must be reported to the police and State Insurance Company.

Border crossing

All visitors must present their passports at the border between the Czech Republic and Slovakia.

Carriage of children

Children under 12 and less than 4ft 9in (150cm) in height, are not allowed to travel on the front seat.

Drinking and driving

Do not drink and drive. No degree of alcohol in the blood is tolerated.

Fuel

Petrol stations on international roads and in main towns are open 24 hours a day.
Leaded petrol: Regular (90 octane) and Super (96 octane) available.
Unleaded petrol: Super (95 octane) available; pump legend *Natural*. Maps showing outlets for unleaded petrol are issued at border crossings.
Diesel: widely available.
Credit cards: accepted by some petrol stations in main towns and tourist areas.

Lighting

Foglights may be used in case of fog, snow or heavy rain. If the vehicle is not equipped with foglights, the driver must use dipped headlights in these conditions. Motorcyclists must use dipped headlights at all times. At level crossings, waiting vehicles should emit sidelights only.

Orange Badge holders

There are special parking spaces for cars used by disabled drivers. Permits issued abroad are accepted in Slovakia.

Overtaking

Overtaking regulations conform with international usage. Trams are overtaken on the right, unless there is no space, when it is permitted to overtake on the left. However in Bratislava, it is prohibited to overtake trams on the left and the driver must follow the tram until he has enough room to pass on the right. Drivers must not overtake near a tram refuge.

Parking

In a one-way street, parking is permitted on the left side only. Stopping and parking are prohibited in all places where visibility is poor or where the vehicle could cause an obstruction; in particular, near an intersection, pedestrian crossing, bus or tram stop, level crossing and alongside a tram line unless there is still 3.5 metre wide side lane free. In Bratislava, parking is restricted in many places. Parking meters are being introduced in Bratislava and Kosice. Wheel clamps are also in use.

Priority

At uncontrolled crossroads or road intersections not marked by a priority sign, priority must be given to vehicles coming from the right. Drivers may not enter the intersection unless their exit is clear. A tram turning right and crossing the line of a vehicle on its right has priority once the driver has signalled his intention to turn.

Road signs

Most conform to the international pattern. Other road signs which may be seen are:
Prujezd zakazany: closed to all vehicles
Jednosmerny premavka: one-way traffic
Dialkova premavka: by-pass
Obchadzka: diversion
H nemocnica: hospital
Chodte vlavo: pedestrians must walk on the left.

Seat belts

If fitted, compulsory use in front and rear seats.

Signalling

Horns may be used only to warn other road users in case of danger or to signify intention to overtake. Warning may also be given by flashing the headlights. In Bratislava, the use of the horn is prohibited.

Speed limits

Built-up areas: 30mph (50kmh); outside built-up areas: 56mph (90kmh); motorways: 68mph (110kmh). Car and caravan/trailer 50mph (80kmh). The maximum speed limit for motorcyclists outside built up areas on all roads is 56mph (90kmh). Minimum speed on motorways is 31mph (50kmh).

Tolls

See page 79.

Traffic offences

Cash on-the-spot fines of up to 2000 SK are imposed.

General information

Banks

Open Mon-Fri 0830-1630. Closed Sat.

Currency

Slovak crown (SK) divided into 100 hellers.

Museums

Open Tue-Sat 1000-1700. Closed Mon.

Castles

Castles are usually open from 1 May to 31 August. Open Tue-Sat, 0900-1600/1800. Closed Mon.

Public holidays

New Year's Day; Easter Monday; May Day; National Liberation Day, 8 May; St Cyril and St Method, 5 July; Johannes Hus Festival Day, 6 July; Independence Day, 28 October; Christmas 24-26 Dec.

Shops

Food shops open Mon-Fri 0800-1800, Sat 0800-1200. Department stores open Mon-Fri 0800/0900-1900 (Thu 2000), Sat 0800-1500.

Visa

British Nationals no longer require a visa.

Slovenia

Motoring information

National motoring organisation

Avto-Moto Zveza Slovenije, FIA, Dunajska 128, 61113 Ljubljana. Tel: 61-341 341.

Accidents and emergencies

Police Tel: 113, Fire Brigade Tel: 112, Ambulance Tel: 112.

In the event of an accident, the police must be called. A visitor must obtain a certificate from the police, detailing damage to the vehicle, in order to facilitate export from the country.

Carriage of children

Children under 12 are not allowed to travel on the front seat.

Drinking and driving

The blood alcohol legal limit is 50mg.

Fuel

Service stations at entry points and on motorways are open 24 hours, otherwise 0700-2000 Monday to Saturday.
Leaded petrol: Super (98 octane) available.
Unleaded petrol: 91 and 95 octane available from most service stations.
Credit cards: accepted at some petrol stations.
Spare fuel: importation of spare fuel is prohibited.

Lighting

Spare bulbs must be carried. Motorcyclists must use headlights day and night.

Orange Badge holders

Disabled persons in possession of a blue and white badge may park in places for the disabled. Similar foreign badges with the international symbol of the wheelchair are generally recognised, although there are no official regulations in force.

Seat belts

If fitted, compulsory use in front and rear seats.

Speed limits

Motorcycle, car, car and caravan: in built-up areas the limit is 37mph (60kmh); outside built-up areas 50mph (80kmh). Motorways, motorcycles and cars, 75mph (120kmh); cars and caravans, 50mph (80kmh).

Tolls

See page 79.

Traffic offences

Police are empowered to impose on-the-spot fines which must be paid in the national currency.

General information

Banks

Open Mon-Fri 0800-1800, Sat 0800-1200.

Currency

The currency is the Tolar. Foreign currency may be exchanged at all international border crossings, and in all major towns at tourist agencies, hotels and banks.

Photography

It is prohibited to take photographs in sensitive areas, eg railways, airports, bridges, etc.

Public holidays

1, 2 Jan; Culture Day, 8 Feb; Easter Monday; Resistance Day, 27 April: Labour Days, 1, 2 May; Statehood Day 25 June; Assumption Day, 15 Aug, Reformation Day, 31 Oct; Remembrance Day, 1 Nov; Christmas 25 Dec; Independence Day, 26 Dec.

Shops

Open Mon-Fri 0730-1900, Sat 0730-1300.

Tourist office

Slovenian Tourist Office, 49 Conduit Street, London, W1R 9PB. Tel: 0171 734 4630.

Spain

Motoring information

National motoring organisation

Real Automóvil Club de España (RACE), José Abascal 10, 28003 Madrid. Tel: 447 3200. Office hours: Mon–Thur 0830–1730 Fri 0830–1430.

Accidents and emergencies

In the case of an emergency in Madrid, Barcelona or other main town, Police Tel: 091, medical assistance Tel: 092, Fire Brigade Tel: 080. Elsewhere consult the telephone directory. The Traffic Control Department operates an assistance service for road accidents, including a telephone network on motorways and some other roads. Drivers in need of assistance should ask the operator for *auxilio en carretera*.

Carriage of children

Children under 12 travelling in the front of a vehicle must be seated in an approved child seat, otherwise they must be seated in the rear of a vehicle.

Drinking and driving

The blood alcohol legal limit is 50mg.

Fuel

Leaded petrol: Regular (92 octane) and Super (97 octane) available.
Unleaded petrol: Regular (95 octane) available; pump legend *gasolina sin plomo*.
Most readily found at the popular tourist resorts between Costa del Sol and Costa Brava, at Autopista service areas, and in the Burgos-Bilbao area.
Diesel: available; pump legend *gasóleo*
Credit cards: accepted at some petrol stations.
Spare fuel: 10 litres of petrol in a can may be imported duty free.

Glasses

Motorists who wear glasses for driving should ensure that a spare pair is carried in the vehicle.

Internal ferries

Compania Transmediterranea SA operate all-year car ferry services to the Balearic and Canary Islands on the following routes:
Balearic Islands:
Barcelona/Valencia to Palma (Mallorca), Mahón (Menorca) and Ibiza. There is an inter-island service from Palma to Mahón and Ibiza.
Canary Islands:
Cádiz to Las Palmas (Gran Canaria) and Santa Cruz (Tenerife).
Inter-island services to Fuerteventura, Lanzarote, Gomera, Hierro and La Palma. UK agent for reservations and tickets: Southern Ferries, 179 Piccadilly, London W1V 9DB, Tel: 0171-491 4968.

Lighting

The use of dipped headlights is compulsory at night on motorways and fast roads, even if well lit.

Motorcycles must use lights at all times. Motor vehicles must have lights on in tunnels. A spare set of light bulbs must be carried.

Mirrors

Temporarily imported vehicles should have a minimum of two rear-view mirrors. Drivers must have a clear rear view of at least 50 m, caravans should be equipped with extension mirrors.

Orange Badge holders

Most large towns operate their own schemes but types of badges and concessions provided are not standardised. It is understood, however, badge holders from other countries would be shown consideration.

Overtaking

Outside built-up areas, signal your intention to overtake by sounding your horn in the daytime or by flashing headlights at night.
When overtaking, use your indicators. The driver of a commercial vehicle will switch on his nearside flashing indicator when he thinks it is safe for you to overtake (the one next to the right-hand verge). If there is danger ahead, he will switch off and flash his offside light until the road is clear. Stationary trams may not be overtaken when passengers are boarding or alighting.

Parking

Usual restrictions on parking apply.
On uneven dates in one-way streets in towns, vehicles should be parked on the side of the road where the houses bear uneven numbers. On the side where houses bear even numbers, parking is allowed on even dates.
Park facing the same direction as the traffic flow on that side.
Parking meters and traffic wardens operate in Madrid and Barcelona. Blue Zones, *zona azul*, are indicated by signs. Maximum period of parking between 0800 and 2100 is 1½ hours. Discs are available from hotels, town halls and travel agencies. In the centre of some large towns there is a *zona ORA* where parking is allowed only against tickets bought in tobacconists; tickets are valid for 30, 60 or 90 minutes.
Vehicles parked against regulations may be removed.

Pedestrian crossings

Jay walking is not permitted. In main towns pedestrians may not cross a road unless a traffic light is at red against the traffic, or a policeman gives permission. Offenders can be fined on the spot.

Priority

Traffic coming from the right has priority. When entering a major road from a minor one, where there is normally a sign *Stop* or *Ceda el Paso* (give way), traffic from both directions on the major road has priority.
Trams and emergency vehicles always have priority.

Road signs

Ceda el Paso: give way
Cuidado: take care
Obras: roadworks
Peligro: danger

Signalling

Do warn road users of your whereabouts by horn or light signals. Do not make unnecessary use of horns. In urban areas horns may only be used in an emergency.

Speed limits

Built-up areas: 31mph (50kmh); outside built-up areas: 56–62mph (90–100kmh); motorways: 74mph (120kmh).
In residential areas the maximum speed is 12mph (20kmh). To overtake outside built-up areas, it is permitted to increase speed limits by 12mph (20kmh). Cars towing a caravan or trailer, 50mph (80kmh) on dual carriageways and motorways, 44mph (70kmh) on other roads.

Tolls

Payable on certain roads (see page 79).

Traffic lights

As in the UK, but two red lights mean 'No Entry'.

Traffic offences

Police can impose on-the-spot fines of up to 100,000 Ptas. A fine can be contested within 15 days. Visiting motorists must pay immediately unless they can give the name of a person or company in Spain who will guarantee payment, otherwise the vehicle will be impounded until the fine is paid. However, except in certain cases, there is a standard reduction in the fine of 20% for immediate settlement. A *Boletin de Denuncia* is issued specifying the offence and the amount of the fine.
Check that the amount written tallies with the amount paid.
There are instructions in English on the back of the form for an appeal.
Make this within ten days – do not delay until your return home. You may write in English.
If the police take no action about your protest, that is the end of the matter.

General information

Banks

Open Mon–Fri 0900–1400, Sat 0900–1300 in some towns.

Currency

Peseta.

Museums

Tue–Sat 0900/1000–1300/1400 and 1500/1600–1800/2000. Sun 0900/1000–1400. Entry to state museums is free on Saturdays, after 1430 on Sundays and on 18 May, 6 Dec and 12 Dec.

Public holidays

New Year's Day; Epiphany; St Joseph's Day, 19 Mar*; Maundy Thursday*; Good Friday; Easter Monday; Labour Day; St James's Day, 25 July*; Assumption 15 Aug; National Day, 12 Oct; All Saints Day, 1 Nov; Constitution Day, 6 Dec; Immaculate Conception, 8 Dec; Christmas Day.
*not observed in all provinces.

Shops

Open Mon–Sat 0900/1000–1300/1330 and 1500/1530–1930/2000.

Tourist office

Spanish Tourist Office, 57–58 St James's Street, London SW1A 1LD, Tel: 0891-669920 (calls cost 60p per minute at all times).
Official website: www.tourspain.es

Sweden

Motoring information

National motoring organisation

Kungl Automobil Klubben (KAK), FIA, Södra Balsieholmshamnen 16, 111 48 Stockholm. Tel: 8-678 00 51. Office hours: Mon–Thurs 0900–1600, Fri 0900–1300.

Accidents and emergencies

Police, Fire Brigade and Ambulance Tel: 112. Do not leave the scene of an accident.

Breakdowns

In the case of breakdown, contact the alarm service (*Larmtjänst*), Tel: (020) 910 040.

Carriage of children

Children aged seven or under should be seated in a special child restraint, or in a seat which allows them to use normal seat belts.

Climbing lanes

A climbing lane in Sweden is an extra lane sometimes provided on steep hills to the right of the regular lane.
It allows overtaking of slow-moving vehicles and merges with the regular lane a short way past the end of the climb. These are not as slow lanes in other countries.

Drinking and driving

The blood alcohol legal limit is 20mg.

Fuel

The normal opening hours of petrol stations are 0700–1900. In most cities, near motorways and on main roads, petrol stations remain open until 2000/2200 or even 24 hours.
Outside open hours, petrol stations have automatic pumps (*sedel automat*) which accept bank notes. Self-serve pumps – *Tanka Själv*.
Leaded petrol: low-lead 96 octane called 'Normal' and super 98 octane called 'Premium' both grades contain a lead additive for cars unable to use unleaded petrol.

Unleaded petrol: 95 octane, pump legend *Blyfrei 95*, 98 octane, pump legend *Blyfre 98* (not sold at all petrol stations). Both fuels dispensed from green pumps.
Diesel: rarely available at self-service pumps. Ideally, diesel should be purchased during normal working hours.
Credit cards: generally accepted, but at 24-hour service stations on main roads/ in major towns, you must pay with 20 or 100 Crown notes.
Spare fuel: motorists are allowed to carry up to 30 litres in cans. Petrol imported in spare cans is subject to payment of duty/VAT.

Lighting

All motor vehicles must use dipped headlights day and night all year round.

Motorways

There are no petrol stations or service areas on motorways, however facilities are signposted at motorway exits.

Orange Badge holders

Badge holders may park as follows:
– for 3 hours where parking is banned or allowed only for a shorter period by local regulation
– for up to 24 hours where a time limit of 3 hours or more is in force
– in reserved parking spaces indicated by signs with the international symbol, for no longer than the permitted time.
In general, parking charges must be paid but there may be local exemptions. The local police can give further information. Where parking is prohibited for special reasons such as taxi zones or loading areas, it is not possible to park even if you are a badge holder. If a disabled parking badge lacks the international symbol, a temporary Swedish badge can be issued by the local community.

Overtaking

Many roads in Sweden have wide shoulders – if you are driving slower than other traffic, or if you are driving a very wide vehicle, you are allowed to move out onto the shoulder to make it easier for other people to overtake you, but do not use the shoulder as another traffic lane.
If you drive onto the shoulder, give way to vehicles

behind you before driving back onto the road again, as you will be held responsible for any accident.

Do not force another vehicle onto the shoulder if you wish to overtake it – no vehicle is obliged to move onto the shoulder.

Some narrow roads have warning lines – long markings at short intervals, instead of unbroken lines.

These mean that visibility is limited in one or both directions. Cross a warning line safely to pass a pedestrian, a cyclist, a stationary/slow-moving vehicle.

Trams should be overtaken on the right if the position of the tracks so permit. If there is no refuge at a tram stop, stop and give way to passengers boarding and alighting. There are trams in Göteborg, Malmo and Norrköping.

Parking

Vehicles parked on the carriageway must be on the right-hand side of the road. If in doubt about local regulations ask the police.

Do not park or stop on motorways or arterial roads other than in the parking areas provided. Do observe local parking restrictions.

Maps showing parking regulations in Stockholm and some other towns may be obtained from the motoring organisations or through the local authority concerned.

Parking meters are in use in larger towns, usually from 0800 to 1800. The permitted parking time varies (usually two hours) and is always indicated on the meter. Parking fees vary according to locality, usually 5–10 SEK per hour.

Fines are imposed for illegal parking.

Pedestrian crossings

Do give pedestrians the right of way on a pedestrian crossing. Pedestrians must use official crossings. It is an offence for them to cross the road against a red light.

Priority

Give way to vehicles already on a priority road before you enter it, also when you leave a petrol station, car park, camping site, or similar area.

At other road junctions give way to traffic coming from the right, unless there is a road sign to the contrary.

When turning left give way to oncoming traffic.

When you see a 'Stop' sign, you must stop at a point where you can see up and down the other road (usually at the stop line), give way to any traffic approaching along it.

At most roundabouts, traffic already on the roundabout has priority (clearly indicated by signposting). Give trams priority.

Signalling

Do give warning of your approach by using the horn, or by light signals, where this is necessary to prevent an accident. In built-up areas, do not give audible warning, unless it is essential to prevent an accident.

Speed limits

Built-up areas: 31mph (50kmh) lower limit of 20mph (30kmh) applies in residential areas as indicated on signs; outside built-up areas: 44mph (70kmh); on good roads, motorways and semi-motorways, a speed limit of 56mph (90kmh) or 68mph (110kmh) is permitted for cars according to signs. Car and trailer/caravan with effective braking system, 50mph (80kmh).

Traffic offences

Swedish police are authorised to impose, but not collect, fines on the spot for violation of traffic regulations. Fines range from 300 to 1,200 SEK, but if two or more offences are committed and total fines exceed 2,500 SEK, the offender will be taken to court.

Fineable offences: registration plate dirty/missing; driving without lights in daylight; exceeding the speed limit; not having a warning triangle or GB plate.

General Information

Banks

Open 0930–1500. City centres open until 1800.

Currency

Swedish crown (SEK).

Museums

Opening hours vary but are generally 0930/1000 –1500/1600. Most museums closed Mondays.

Public holidays

New Year's Day; Epiphany; Good Friday; Easter Monday; Labour Day; Ascension; Whit Sunday; Whit Monday; Midsummer (Sat between 20 and 26 June); All Saints, (Sat between 31 Oct and 6 Nov); Christmas, 24, 25, 26 Dec.

Shops

Open Mon–Fri 0900–1800, Sat 0900–1300/1600, although hours vary throughout the week. In some large towns, department stores remain open until 1900/2000.

Tourist office

Swedish Travel and Tourism Council, 11 Montagu Place, London W1H 2AL, Tel: 0171-724 5868 Official website: www.gosweden.org

Switzerland

Motoring information

National motoring organisation

Automobile Club de Suisse (ACS), FIA, 39 Wasserwerkgasse, 3000 Bern 13. Tel: (031) 328 31 11. Office hours: Mon–Fri 0800–1200 and 1400–1730.

Accidents and emergencies

Police Tel: 117, Fire Brigade Tel: 118, Ambulance Tel: 144.

Carriage of children

Children under seven years of age may not travel in the front seat, unless an approved child restraint is fitted.

Drinking and driving

The blood alcohol legal limit is 80mg.

Fuel

On motorways, service stations are usually open 0600-2200/2400, with the exception of Basel North, Pratteln North/South, and Coldrerio East/West (N2) which are open 24 hours. On normal roads, usual opening hours are 0600/0700–2000; smaller stations are open 0700/0800–1800.
Petrol is widely available from 24-hour automatic pumps, which accept 10 or 20 SF notes.
Leaded petrol: Super (98 octane) available.
Unleaded petrol: Super (95 octane) available; pump legend *bleifrei*, *essence sans plomb* or *benzina sensa piomba*.
Diesel: available.
Credit cards: accepted. Spare fuel: 25 litres of petrol in a can may be imported duty free.

Internal ferries

A car ferry operates across Lake Lucerne between Beckenreid and Gersau (April–October), and across Lake Zürich between Horgen and Meilen (all year). There are also international ferry services to Germany across Lake Constance (Bodensee) from Romanshorn to Frederichshafen and from Constance to Meersburg.

Lighting

Do use sidelights after nightfall or in thick fog if the vehicle is stationary, except if parked where there is sufficient street lighting, or in an authorised car park. Dipped headlights are compulsory in tunnels. Motorcyclists should use lights at all times.

Motorways

Signposted in green. All vehicles using the motorway network must display a vignette (see page 80). Motel accommodation is available at a number of locations on the network.

Mountain roads

Take extra care when travelling on mountain roads. You must be able to pull up within half the distance of clear vision, especially when negotiating a blind bend. When two vehicles meet on a narrow mountain road, the descending car must keep to the extreme right-hand side of the road and even stop or go into reverse if necessary. Mountain postal roads are indicated by a sign with a post-horn in yellow on a blue rectangle. Here, postal vehicles have priority. The same sign with a red diagonal stripe indicates the end of the postal road. Pull up if signalled to do so by postal coach drivers.

A sign showing a disc with a wheel and chains in the centre indicates that snow chains are necessary for the mountain road ahead. Some mountain postal roads are one-way only. This is indicated by a white rectangle beneath the blue rectangle with the yellow horn. On others during certain hours, one-way single file traffic is in operation. Circulation hours in both directions are posted at each end of the road.

Orange Badge holders

Badge holders are allowed to park as follows:
– for 4 hours over the permitted parking time where parking is restricted to 20 minutes or more
– for 2 hours where parking is banned, provided other traffic is not restricted or endangered

These concessions only apply if there is no public or private parking place with unlimited parking time available to the public in the immediate vicinity. Badge holders must also observe any police restrictions, private parking places regulations, traffic rights of way, parking time limits less than 20 minutes and no stopping zones.

Reserved parking places indicated by signs with the international symbol are provided for disabled people. Concessions at parking meters vary from town to town and badge holders should enquire at a local police station to see if any are available.

Overtaking

Overtake on the left. When overtaking, it is compulsory to signal right before returning to the right-hand lane. A moving tram must be overtaken on the right if there is sufficient room; if not, the vehicle may be overtaken on the left. Overtake a stationary tram or train on the right only if there is a refuge. If not, overtake on the left only if there is no danger to traffic.

Motorcyclists must not overtake a column of vehicles or weave between vehicles.

Parking

Do not park where there is a sign *Stationierungsverbot* or *Interdiction de Stationner* or where parking might hinder traffic. Motorists with parking discs may park in Blue Zones free. Parking discs can be obtained free from ACS and TCS offices, and in Basel, Bern and Genève discs

can be obtained from most petrol stations, garages, kiosks, restaurants and police stations. Immobolise your vehicle by leaving it in bottom or reverse gear, by use of a chock or by turning the front wheels towards the kerb. Wheel clamps may be used on illegally parked vehicles. Parking on pavements is forbidden unless authorised by signs. Murren, Wengen, Zermatt, Braunwald and Rigi are inaccessible by car (park at railway stations and complete your journey by public transport).

Priority

Main roads are marked by a white centre line. If the road is clear, you can cross a broken white line when overtaking or turning left. Do not cross a double white line. In open country, main road traffic has right of way over that entering from secondary roads. In built-up areas, traffic from the right has priority. Trams have right of way on all roads. An international priority sign is placed on most secondary highways where they intersect with main roads having priority. Blue posts indicate a main road. In built-up areas, buses have priority when leaving a bus-stop.

Signalling

Use a horn with consideration in residential areas. After dark, use your headlamp flasher instead, unless there is an emergency.

Speed limits

Built-up areas: 31mph (50kmh); outside built-up areas: 50mph (80kmh); motorways: 62–74mph (100–120kmh).
Cars towing a caravan or trailer: up to 1000kg, 50mph (80kmh); over 1000kg, 37mph (60kmh) and 50mph (80kmh) on motorways.

Temporary importation of caravans

Caravans and trailers not exceeding 2.30 metres in width and 8 metres in length may be imported without formality. Caravans up to 2.50 metres wide may enter Switzerland if they are towed by a four-wheel drive vehicle or by a vehicle exceeding 3.5 tonnes: the total length of the combination must not exceed 18 metres. No authorisation is required.

Touring information

General information, Tel: 111; weather reports, Tel: 162; mountain pass conditions, Tel: 163.

Traffic offences

Police are empowered to impose and collect on-the-spot fines for traffic offences.

General information

Banks

Generally open Mon–Fri 0830–1630. In Lausanne, banks close 1230–1330.

Currency

Swiss franc.

Public holidays

New Year's Day; Good Friday; Easter Monday; Ascension; Whit Monday; Christmas Day.

Shops

Open Mon–Fri 0800/0900–1830 (1845 in Genève), Sat 0800–1600/1700.

Tourist office

Switzerland Tourism, Swiss Centre, Swiss Court, London W1V 8EE, Tel: 0171-734 1921
Official website: www.switzerlandtourism.ch

Turkey

Motoring information

National motoring organisation

Türkiye Turing Ve Otomobil Kurumu (TTOK), FIA, 1, Oto Sanay Sitesi Yani, Seyrantepe, 4 Levent, Istanbul. Tel: 212 282 81 40. Office hours: Mon-Fri 0830-1200 and 1230-1700.

Accidents and emergencies

Police Tel: 155, Fire Brigade Tel: 110, Ambulance Tel: 112. All accidents (whether there are injuries caused or not) must be reported to the police as a report has to be prepared by them for the Turkish Insurance Bureau.

Carriage of children

It is advisable for children to travel in the back seat of the vehicle.

Crash helmets

Compulsory for motorcyclists.

Drinking and driving

The blood alcohol legal limit is 50mg.

Drivers

Normally, only those 18 and over may drive but visitors holding a valid full driving licence in their country of residence, may do so even if they are under 18. They may, however, only drive foreign-registered vehicles.

Fuel

Motorists are advised to 'top-up' their tanks at every opportunity.
Leaded petrol: Regular (91 octane) and Super (96 octane) available.
Unleaded petrol: Super (95 octane) available; pump legend *kursunsuz benzin*.
Diesel: available.
Credit cards: not widely accepted. Spare fuel: 25 litres maximum in cans may be imported duty free.

Lighting

Dipped headlights must be used after sunset in built-up areas. A vehicle parked at the roadside after dark must display sidelights, whether or not the road is lit. However, this does not apply in built-up areas if the vehicle is visible from a distance of 150 metres.

Overtaking

Do not overtake at intersections, level crossings, curves, on bridges, in tunnels or where road signs indicate that it is forbidden.

Parking

The sign *Park Yapilmaz* indicates that parking is forbidden. Parking is not permitted on pedestrian crossings, outside garage/car park entrances, on tramways, near intersections or bends, on level crossings, underpasses, overpasses or within 25 metres of danger signs.

Priority

Except where otherwise indicated, priority must be given to vehicles coming from the right. Vehicles on a main road have priority over those entering from a secondary road.

Road signs

Most signs conform to the international pattern, but other road signs which may be seen are:
Dikkat: attention
Dur: stop
Gümrük: Customs
Hastahane: hospital
Park Yapilmaz: no parking
Tamirat: roadworks
Yavas: slow
The word 'Nufus' (inhabitants) often appears on signs at the entrance into towns to indicate the population. 'Rakim' indicates the altitude.

Seat belts

If fitted, compulsory in front and rear seats.

Signalling

Use of the horn is forbidden unless absolutely necessary.

Speed limits

Built-up areas: 31mph (50kmh); outside built-up areas: 56mph (90kmh). Motorways 81mph (130kmh). Cars towing a caravan or trailer are limited to 25mph (40kmh) in built-up areas, and 44mph (70kmh) on all other roads.

Temporary importation of vehicles

Vehicle details will be entered in the visitor's passport. The vehicle must be exported by that person. If a vehicle is imported by a person other than the owner, a letter of authorisation from the owner must be held by the driver and certified either by a lawyer or RAC.

Tolls

See page 80.

Traffic offences

Police are empowered to impose on-the-spot fines for violations of traffic regulations.

General information

Banks

Open Mon-Fri 0830-1200 and 1330-1700.

Currency

Turkish lira.

Museums

Open Tue-Sun 0830-1200 and 1330-1700 (winter), 0830-1730 (summer).

Photography

Photography is forbidden in certain areas as indicated by signs Yasak Bolge or Yabancilara Yasaktir.

Public holidays

New Year's Day; Seker Bayrami religious festival (moveable in March); Independence and Children's Day, 23 Apr; Youth, Sports and Atatürk Commemoration Day, 19 May; Kurban Bayrami religious festival (moveable in June); Victory Day, 30 Aug; Republic Day, 29 Oct.

Shops

Open Mon-Sat 0930-1300 and 1400-1900. Tourist shops operate similar hours.

Visa

British nationals visiting Turkey for less than three months must purchase a visa (costing £10), on arrival at the airport or frontier. Visitors are advised to provide new £ Sterling banknotes in payment.

Tourist office

Turkish Embassy Information Counsellor's Office, First floor, 170-173 Piccadilly, London W1V 9DD. Tel: 0171 355 4207.

United Kingdom

Motoring Information

National Motoring Organisation

RAC Motoring Services (RAC), FIA. Registered office: 1 Forest Road, Feltham, TW13 7RR. Tel: Roadside service (RAC Members only) 0800 82 82 82. UK traffic and travel information 0891 347 333 (calls cost 60p per minute at all times. Calls from mobile phones may be charged more).

Carriage of children

Children under 3 years of age must be carried in an approved child restraint. Children under the age of 1 year can be safely carried in the front passenger seat in an approved baby carrier. However, in vehicles fitted with a front passenger airbag, baby carriers should be installed in the rear seats.

Drinking and driving

The blood alcohol legal limit is 80mg.

Ferry services in the United Kingdom

The main ferry routes from the United Kingdom mainland to its islands and the Channel Islands are outlined below, together with the reservations telephone numbers.
Channel Islands
Poole – Guernsey/Jersey, operated by Condor Fast Ferries. Tel: 01305 761551.
Isle of Wight
Portsmouth – Fishbourne; Lymington – Yarmouth, operated by Wightlink. Tel: 0990 827744.
Southampton – Cowes, operated by Red Funnel. Tel: 01703 334010.
Isle of Man
Heysham/Liverpool – Douglas, operated by Isle of Man Steam Packet Co. Tel 0990 523523.
Scottish Islands
Aberdeen – Lerwick (Shetland); Scrabster – Stromness (Orkney), operated by P&O Scottish Ferries. Tel: 01224 572615.
Numerous Clyde and Western Isle routes are operated by Caledonian MacBrayne. Tel: 0990 650000.

Lighting

The use of headlights is compulsory in darkness and at times of poor visibility such as fog, snow and rain.

Motorway assistance

Motorway marker posts are situated 100 metres apart, with an arrow pointing towards the nearest SOS telephone and giving the distance in hundreds of metres. They also have a unique number to identify the location of your vehicle to the police or RAC.

Orange Badge holders

The Orange Badge scheme provides parking concessions to persons with severe walking difficulties who travel as drivers or passengers. The scheme does not apply in Central London, on road systems at some airports such as London Heathrow or on private roads. Access to certain town centres may be prohibited or limited to vehicles with special permits.
Persons who think they may be entitled to a badge should apply to the Social Services Departments of their County, Metropolitan District or London Borough Council in England and Wales. In Scotland applications should be made to The Chief Executive of their Regional or Island Council.

Seat belts

In cars and MPVs, seat belts where fitted, must be worn by front and rear seat occupants.

Speed limits

Built up areas: 30mph on roads with street lighting 200 yards apart or less, unless another speed limit is signed; outside built up areas: the national speed limit on motorways and dual carriageways is 70mph and on other roads it is 60mph. Roads with lower limits will be marked by speed limit signs.

Tolls

There are no toll roads in the United Kingdom, excepting some bridges, tunnels and private roads. The principal tolls are as follows:
M25 east of London – Dartford Tunnel/Queen Elizabeth II Bridge: private car £1.00;

M4 and M48 near Bristol – Severn Bridges
(westbound only): private car £4.20;
A38 near Plymouth – Tamar Bridge (eastbound
only): private car £1.00;
A477 near Pembroke Dock – Cleddau Bridge:
private car 75p;
A15/A63 near Hull – Humber Bridge: private car
£1.90;
A5139 & A5030 Liverpool – Kingsway and
Queensway Tunnels: private car £1.00;
A19 near Newcastle – Tyne Tunnel: private car 65p;
M898/A82 near Glasgow – Erskine Bridge; any
vehicle 60p;
A90/M90 near Edinburgh – Forth Road Bridge
(northbound only); private car 80p;
A92 near Dundee – Tay Bridge (southbound only):
private car 80p;
A87 Isle of Skye – Skye Bridge: private car £4.30
low season and £5.20 high season.

Traffic offences

Motoring offences may be dealt with in a variety of
ways depending on their nature and severity and
the legal penalty.
Verbal warnings – police have wide discretion to
use this power.
Vehicle Defect Rectification Scheme (VDRS) – a
police officer discovering a single, minor vehicle
defect can, instead of prosecuting, require the
driver to rectify it and produce evidence of this at
a police station within 14 days.
Fixed penalty notice – police officers, traffic
wardens and local authority parking attendants
can issue a fixed penalty notice as an alternative
to summons.
Summons – the more serious traffic offences and
alleged offences where the driver refuses the
alternative offered, or has 9 or more points on their
licence, will be dealt with by summons at a
Magistrates Court.

Yugoslavia

At the time of going to print travel is not
recommended in Yugoslavia.

General Information

Embassy

Embassy of the Federal Republic of Yugoslavia
5-7 Lexham Gardens, London W8 5JJ.
Tel: 0171 370 6105.

Toll roads & bridges

Toll charges are correct at the time of going to press, details for certain countries are selective. A leaflet for countries marked (*) is available from RAC Travel Information, Tel: 0891 347 333 (calls charged at 60p per minute).

Austria*

A motorway tax disc must be displayed on all vehicles using motorways.
Visitors may purchase a weekly (valid for a maximum of 10 days) or monthly (valid for two consecutive calendar months) disc at all major Austrian border crossings, petrol stations and post offices.
Annual discs are also available.
The cost, in Austrian Schillings, is as follows:

	2 month	weekly
motorcycle	80	not available
private car, certain		
mini-buses	150	70
vehicle (3.5-7.5 t)	1500	300

(1) Disc is not valid on S16 Arlberg Tunnel, A13 Brenner Motorway, A9 Pyhrn Motorway, A10 Tauern Motorway (although it entitles motorists to a 15% discount on the toll).

Major Austian toll road companies issue multiple journey cards, which allow an appreciable reduction in the price charged for a single journey. An additional charge may be made per person for over two or three people in cars or minibuses, but children travel at reduced prices, or free. Tolls are in Austrian Schillings. Credit cards not accepted.

AUSTRIA–ITALY
Timmelsjoch High Alpine Road

motorcycle	single	50
	return	70
car	single	80
	return	120

(no trailers or caravans permitted)

TYROL–ITALY
Brenner motorway (A13)

motorcycle	100
car, motor caravan, minibus (9 seats)	110
car with caravan or trailer	150

KITZBUHEL–EAST TYROL
Felber Tauern Rd

motorcycle	110
car (with or without caravan) motor caravan	
minibus (up to 9 seats), summer/winter	140/130

SALZBURG–TYROL
Gerlos Road

motorcycle	50
car with or without trailer	90

Grossglockner Pass

motorcycle	230
car	350
car and caravan/trailer, motor caravan	350

BLUDENZ–LANDECK
Silvretta High Alp Rd

motorcycle	140
private car per person	150
motor caravan	240

(caravans/trailers prohibited)

SALZBURG–CARINTHIA
Tauern motorway (A10)

motorcycle	100
car, motorcaravan, minibus (9 seats)	140
caravan or trailer	40

Bulgaria

Tolls are levied on foreign registered vehicles using motorways and dual carriageways as follows:

	entry tax	road tax per km
car, van and mini bus	US$10	US$0.10

Bulgaria/Romania

A toll and environmental tax is levied to use the bridge across the river Danube between Rousse in Bulgaria and Gjourguevo (Giurgia) in Romania. The following rates apply to foreign registered vehicles: (Correct 1997 and subject to increase).

motorcycle	60 leva
private car	210 leva
minibus with up to 11 seats including the driver	390 leva

Environmental tax

private car	US$ 1 or DM 2
minibus	US$ 2 or DM 3.50

Croatia

Tolls are payable on the following motorway sections. Current tariffs are available from RAC.

E59	Zagreb – Karlovac
E59	Zagreb – Gubasevo
E70	Zagreb – Kutina
E70	Zagreb – N. Gradiska

Czech Republic

Tolls are payable for use of motorways. A sticker, valid for 1 year, must be displayed on the front windscreen. The toll for a car up to 3,500 kg is 800 Kc.

Denmark

Great Belt Link Bridge (Funen to Zealand). Tolls in Danish Kroner

motorcycle	105
car (up to 5 persons)	210
car & caravan/trailer	315

France*

Tolls are payable on most routes, usually by taking a ticket at the point of entry and paying at the exit, although some toll barriers are operated automatically by depositing the exact toll in coins. On numerous sections of autoroute, particularly around cities and large towns, no tolls are levied. Visa and Mastercard are accepted. Tolls in French francs are as follows:

(1) Light motor vehicle with two axles with a height less than 1.30m measured at right angles to the front axle, with or without a luggage trailer; family minibus with up to 9 seats. (Motorcyclists pay a lower rate.)

(2) Vehicle, or vehicle combination (car and trailer/caravan), with more than two axles and a height of not more than 1.30m measured at right angles to the front axle.

(3) Commercial vehicle with two axles with a height of more than 1.30m measured at right angles to the front axle; coach with two axles; motor home; minibus, unless it has a maximum of 9 seats and is for private use, charged as category (1).

Charges correct as of 1 February 1999.

	(1)	(2)	(3)
A1 PARIS–LILLE			
214km			
Autoroute du Nord			
Paris–Roye (Amiens)	36.00	54.00	61.00
Paris–Lille	74.00	110.00	124.00
A2 COMBLES (Jct A1)–BELGIAN FRONTIER			
78km			
Bapaume–Hordain	26.00	40.00	46.00
A4 PARIS–STRASBOURG			
470km			
Autoroute de l'Est			
Paris–Metz	120.00	182.00	211.00
Paris–Strasbourg	183.00	277.00	317.00
Calais–Strasbourg* (617km)			
	233.00	350.00	395.00
A5 PARIS (MELUN)–LANGRES			
247km			
Melun (N104 la Francilienne)–Troyes			
	40.00	46.00	78.00
Troyes–Semoutiers	29.00	33.00	56.00
A6 PARIS–LYON			
456km			
Autoroute du Soleil			
Paris–Beaune	102.00	117.00	194.00
Paris–Lyon	158.00	181.00	300.00
Calais–Lyon*	289.00	382.00	529.00
A7 LYON–MARSEILLE			
313km			
Autoroute du Soleil			
Lyon–Aix–Marseille	115.00	178.00	182.00
Calais–Marseille* (1070 km)			
	394.00	545.00	701.00
A8 AIX-EN-PROVENCE (Coudoux, A7)–NICE– MENTON			
200km			
Autoroute la Provençale			
Aix-en-Provence–Menton			
	100.50	151.00	163.00
Calais–Nice* (1226km)			
	487.00	689.50	845.50

*via A26 Autoroute Les Anglais

A9 ORANGE (A7)–LE PERTHUS
280km
Autoroute
La Languedocienne–Catalane
Orange–Narbonne sud

	78.00	121.00	124.00
Orange–Le Perthus	114.00	178.00	186.00
Calais–Le Perthus* (1235km)			
	486.00	687.00	910.00

A10 PARIS–BORDEAUX
585km
Autoroute l'Aquitaine

Paris–Tours	112.00	169.00	190.00
Paris–Bordeaux	258.00	394.00	432.00
Calais–Bordeaux (870km) (via A16)			
	357.00	543.00	601.00

A11 PARIS–NANTES
383km
Autoroute l'Océane

Paris–Le Mans	90.00	134.00	159.00
Paris–Nantes	173.00	262.00	295.00

A13 PARIS–CAEN
225km
Autoroute de Normandie
Paris (La Défense, A14)–Tancarville (Le Havre)

	77.00	136.00	179.00
Paris (La Défense, A14)–Caen			
	105.00	174.00	216.50

A16 BELGIAN BORDER–CALAIS–BOULOGNE–PARIS
Boulogne–Paris (L'Isle-Adam N1)

	99.00	149.00	169.00

A26 CALAIS–TROYES
400km
Autoroute des Anglais

Calais–Reims	101.00	151.00	168.00
Reims–Troyes	45.00	67.00	90.00

A31 BEAUNE–LUXEMBOURG
364km

Beaune–Dijon	8.00	8.00	15.00
Dijon–Toul	66.00	76.00	126.00

A36 BEAUNE–MULHOUSE
232km
La Comtoise

Beaune–Besançon	35.00	40.00	68.00
Paris–Mulhouse (535 km) (A6/A36)			
	184.00	211.00	351.00

A39 DIJON–DOLE–BOURG EN BRESSE
Crimolois (A31)–Bourg (A40)

	44.00	51.00	84.00

A40 MACON–ST GERVAIS
212km

Macon–St Gervais	105.00	151.00	193.00
Calais–Genève* (842km)			
	337.00	449.00	602.00
Calais–St Gervais* (895km)			
	367.00	502.00	671.00

A41 GRENOBLE–SCIENTRIER
130km

Grenoble–Chambéry	28.00	43.00	43.00
Chambéry–Scientrier (A40)			
	45.00	69.00	69.00

A42 LYON–PONT D'AIN (A40)
64km

	18.00	21.00	34.00

A43/A430 LYON–ALBERTVILLE
150km

Lyon–Les Abrets	32.00	51.00	51.00
Lyon–Albertville	84.00	131.00	131.00

A48 BOURGOIN (A43)–GRENOBLE
49km

Bourgoin–Grenoble	29.00	44.00	44.00
Calais–Grenoble* (860km)			
	340.00	462.00	609.00

A49 GRENOBLE–VALENCE
Tullins–Bourg de Péage

	33.00	51.00	51.00

A50 MARSEILLE–TOULON
62km

	20.00	30.50	32.00

A51 AIX-EN-PROVENCE–SISTERON
103km
Autoroute du Val de Durance
Aix-en-Provence–Sisteron

	46.50	67.50	72.50

*via A26 Autoroute Les Anglais

A52 CHATEAUNEUF-LE-ROUGE (A8)–AUBAGNE (A50)
15km
Aix-en-Provence–Aubagne
| | 17.00 | 25.50 | 27.50 |

A54 ARLES–NIMES OUEST
24km
| | 12.00 | 19.00 | 19.00 |

A57 TOULON–LE CANNET DES MAURES (A8)
| | 21.50 | 32.50 | 35.00 |

A61 TOULOUSE–NARBONNE SUD
150km
Autoroute des Deux-Mers
| | 61.00 | 95.00 | 102.00 |

A62 BORDEAUX–TOULOUSE
244km
Autoroute des Deux-Mers
| | 91.00 | 141.00 | 150.00 |

A63 BORDEAUX–SPANISH FRONTIER
192km
Autoroute de la Côte Basque
St Geours de Maremne–Biriatou
| | 39.50 | 61.00 | 61.00 |

A64 BAYONNE–TARBES–ST GAUDENS (LESTELLE)
218km
La Pyrénéenne
Sames–Tarbes est | 53.00 | 82.00 | 86.00 |
Bayonne–Lestelle | 84.00 | 130.00 | 137.00 |

A71 ORLEANS–CLERMONT FERRAND
293km
Orléans centre–Bourges
| | 48.00 | 76.00 | 83.00 |
Bourges–Clermont Ferrand
| | 68.00 | 78.00 | 129.00 |
Calais–Clermont Ferrand (687km) (via A16)
| | 280.00 | 393.00 | 484.00 |

A72 CLERMONT FERRAND–ST ETIENNE
140km
| | 54.00 | 84.00 | 90.00 |
A81 LE MANS (Joué-en-Charnie)–LAVAL
(La Gravelle) (84km)
| | 47.00 | 71.00 | 84.00 |
Paris–La Gravelle (278km)
| | 145.00 | 215.00 | 251.00 |

A83 NANTES–NIORT
136km
Nantes (La Cour Neuve)–Fontenay-le-Comte
| | 50.00 | 78.00 | 81.00 |

Tolls are charged for crossing the following bridges:
Tancarville Bridge
motorcycle	free
car	15.00 (27.00 return)
car and caravan	19.00
Normandie Bridge (A29)
motorcycle	free
car	33.00 (50.00 return)
car and caravan	38.00

Greece

Tolls are levied on several routes and are given in Drachmas. Tolls are applied as follows:

(1) Motorcycle, scooter
(2) Passenger car; minibus with up to 10 seats
(3) Motor caravan
(4) Car and caravan

	(1)	(2)	(3)	(4)
Athína–Kórinthos	250	500	800	1000
Kórinthos–Pátrai	250	600	1000	1000
Kórinthos –Trípolis	500	900	1200	1500
Athína–Lamí	300	500	800	900
Lamía–Lárisa	250	500	800	1000
Lárisa–Kateríni	250	500	800	1000
Kateríni –Thessalonki	250	500	1000	1000

Hungary

Tolls are payable of the following motorway sections. Current tarriffs are available from RAC.
M1 Gyor to Austrian border (Hegyeshalom)
M3 Budapest – Gyongyar – Fuzesabony
M5 Budapest – Kecskemét

Italy*

Toll tickets are collected on entry to the motorway system and paid on exit. Major credit cards are accepted in payment on the A4, A22, A28 and A32 only. Motorists may pay tolls with a Viacard on the majority of motorways (except A18 and A20). The card can be used for any vehicle and is available in two amounts: 50,000 lire and 90,000 lire. Obtain it from motorway toll booths and services, banks, tourist offices and tobacconists. When leaving a motorway on which the Viacard is accepted, give the card and entry ticket to the attendant who deducts the amount due. At motorway exits with automatic barriers, insert the Viacard into the machine. It is valid until the credit expires. Credit cards are not accepted for payment. Tolls in Lire, as of April 1997, subject to increase in 1999:

(1) Motorcycle; car with a height measured at the front axle of less than 1.30m.
(2) Three-wheeled vehicle; vehicle with a height at the front axle exceeding 1.30m.
(3) Vehicle (with/without trailer) with 3 axles.
(4) Vehicle (with/without trailer) with 4 axles.
(5) Vehicle (with/without trailer) with 5 axles.

	(1)	(2)	(3)	(4)	(5)
A1 MILANO–NAPOLI					
Milano–Bologna	17000	17500	21500	34000	40500
Milano–Roma (ring road)	46500	48000	59000	93000	115000
Milano–Napoli	64000	65500	80500	127000	152000
A3 NAPOLI–REGGIO CALABRIA					
Napoli–Salerno	1600	2000	3500	4500	5000
A4 TORINO–TRIESTE					
Torino–Milano (Ghisolfa)	10000	10500	13000	20500	24500
Milano–Mestre (Venezia)	21500	22000	27000	43000	51500
A5 MONTE BIANCO (Mt. Blanc Tunnel)–TORINO					
Aosta–Torino	18500	20000	27000	42500	49000
Aosta–Santhià (A4)	16000	17500	23500	37000	43000
A6 TORINO–SAVONA (A10)	13500	14000	19000	29500	34500
A7 MILANO–GENOVA	12500	13000	15500	25000	30000
A8/9 MILANO–SESTO CALENDE	3600	3800	4500	7500	8500

A8/9 MILANO–COMO	4200	4300	5000	8500	10000
A10 GENOVA–FRENCH BORDER					
Genova–Savona Vado	4000	4500	5500	8500	10000
Savona Vado–French Border	20000	24000	38500	50000	57500
FIRENZE–PISA	6500	7000	8500	13000	16000
A12 GENOVA–CECINA					
Genove–Rosignano M.	25500	26000	34500	55000	64000
Roma–Citavecchia	5000	5000	7000	11000	13000
A13 BOLOGNA–PADOVA (A4)	9500	10000	12000	19000	23000
A14 BOLOGNA–TARANTO					
Bologna–Pescara (A25)	27000	27500	33500	53500	64000
Bologna–Taranto	60000	61500	75500	119500	143000
A15 PARMA–LA SPEZIA	13500	13500	18500	29000	34000
A16 NAPOLI–CANOSA	22000	22500	27500	43500	52500
A18 MESSINA–CATANIA	5000	6000	9500	13000	15000
A20 MESSINA–PALERMO					
Messina–Furiano	10000	10500	12000	19500	23500
Cefalù–Buonfornello (A19)	1400	1500	1700	3000	3500
A21 TORINO–BRESCIA					
Torino–Piacenza (A1)	14500	15000	18500	29500	35000
Piacenza–Bréscia (A4)	6000	6000	7500	12000	14500
A22 BRENNERO–MODENA					
Brénnero–Verona (A4)	21500	22500	27000	42000	52000
Brénnero–Módena	29000	30000	36500	58000	69500

A23 PALMANOVA–TARVISIO
Udine N.–Tarvisio

8500	8500	10500	17000	20500

A24 ROMA–L'AQUILA–TERAMO

12500	3000	14500	24500	29500

A25 ROMA–PESCARA

14500	15000	17500	28500	34500

A26 GENOVA–ARONA

14500	5000	18500	29000	35000

A27 MESTRE–BELLUNO
Mestre N.–Vittorio Veneto N.

6500	6500	8000	12500	15000

A30 CASERTA–SALERNO

5000	5000	6500	10000	12000

A31 VICENZA–PIOVENE ROCCHETTE

2500	2500	3000	5000	5500

A32 FREJUS TUNNEL–TORINO

14700	17200	27200	36000	42000

Norway

On the E6 west of Oslo, there is a toll charge of 10 Kroner near Drammen.

Portugal*

On the 25 de Abril Bridge, which links Lisboa with the south bank of the River Tagus at the Lisboa end of the Vila Franca de Xira motorway, and Vasco da Gama Bridge, north of Lisboa, toll charges are levied, for most of the year, on northbound traffic only. Tolls, in Escudos, levied on the following *auto-estradas* out of Lisboa. Correct March 1999. Tolls applied as follows:

(1) Motorcycles and vehicles with an axle height less than 1.10m (with or without trailer).
(2) Vehicles with two axles, with an axle height exceeding 1.10m.
(3) Vehicles with three axles, with an axle height exceeding 1.10m.

	(1)	(2)	(3)
A1			
Lisboa–Santarém (64km)	510	890	1150
Santarém–Fatima (49km)	540	960	1230
Fatima–Coimbra (76km)	800	1430	1840

Coimbra–Aveiro (44km	410	730	930
Aveiro–Porto (71km)	610	1060	1390
A2 Lisboa–Grandola (115km)	1230	2160	2780
A3 Porto–Valenca (112km)	1170	2070	2650
A4 Porto–Amarante (53km)	530	970	1240
A5 Lisboa–Cascais (25km)	180	350	350
A6 Marateca–Estremos (103km)	1360	2360	3050
A7 Famalicao PV–Guimarães (21km)			
	210	380	480
A8 Lisboa–Bombarral (63km)	650	1160	1480
A12 Setúbal–Montijo (to Vasco da Gama Bridge) (25km)	650	1160	1480

Slovakia

Tolls are payable for use of certain motorways. A sticker valid for 1 year must be displayed on the front windscreen and for a private car costs 400 or 800 Sk. according to cylinder capacity. Available at border crossings.

Slovenia

Tolls are payable on the following motorway sections.
Current tariffs are available from RAC.

A1/E63 Ljubljana – Kranj
A10/E70 Ljubljana – Razdrto
A10/E57 Maribor – Celje

Spain*

The following tolls, in pesatas, apply to motorcycles and cars (with/without a caravan). Correct October 1997, but subject to increase in 1999.

A1 Burgos (Castañares)–Miranda de Ebro (A68)	1125
A2 Junction A7–Zaragoza (Alfajarin)	2305
A4 Sevilla (Dos Hermanas)–Cadiz (Puerto Real)	1320
A6 Madrid (Villalba)–Adanero	1055
A7 La Jonquera–Barcelona N.	1580
Barcelona S.–Salou	1050
Salou–Valencia (Puzol)	3325
Valencia (Silla)–Alicante (San Juan)	2200
A8 Bilbao (Basauri)–French border (Irun)	1940
A9 La Coruña–Santiago de Compostela	570
Pontevedra–Vigo	405
A15 Pamplona (Noain)–Tudela	1465
A17 Montmelo–Barcelona	260

A18 Barcelona–Manresa	720
A19 Barcelona–Malgrat de Mar (Pallafols)	435
A66 Oveido (Campomanes)–Leon	1265
A68 Bilbao–Zaragoza	4620

Garraf Tunnel (A16) between Barcelona and Sitges)

	610
Vallvidrera Tunnel	360 (410 at peak hours)

Switzerland

In order to drive on Swiss motorways, motorists must buy a vignette. (1999 –SF40).
These can be purchased at Customs posts, post offices, garages, etc. in Switzerland, or in this country from Switzerland Tourism in London.
The vignette is valid for one year, must be displayed on the windscreen and is non-transferable.
A separate vignette must be bought and displayed on a trailer or caravan.
The Swiss advise travellers to buy them in advance to avoid delays and queues at border crossings; credit cards are not accepted for payment of a vignette.
You will be fined 100 Swiss francs if you do not have one, plus the cost of the vignette.

Turkey

Tolls are charged on the following routes:

Edirne – Istanbul	Tsarsus – Pozanti
Istanbul – Izmit	Ankara – Gerede
Gebze – Izmit	Izmir – Çesme

Tolls are levied on the Bosphorus Bridge and Fatih Sultan Mehmet Bridge, payable in the direction Europe to Asia only. The toll for a car is 250,000 TRL.

Tunnels

In many countries it is an offence to drive through a tunnel without headlights. At the exit, police may impose an on-the-spot fine.
*In Austria, vehicles displaying a valid motorway tax disc receive a 15% discount on tunnel tolls.

Albula, Switzerland

Rail tunnel, Thusis, Tiefencastel, Samedan. At least five services daily in each direction.

Rates (in Sw F)

car	85
car with caravan (plus 10–50 per passenger)	140

Arlberg, Austria*

The 14km-long road tunnel is parallel to and south of the Arlberg Pass. When it is closed, vehicle/trailer combinations may be transported through the Arlberg rail tunnel between Langen and St Anton. Make reservations at least three hours before departure of the train, Tel: Langen 05582 201 or St Anton 05446 2242.

Rates (in AS) (road tunnel)

motorcycle	100
car, motor caravan, minibus (up to 9 seats)	130
caravan	60

Bielsa, France/Spain

The 3km-long road tunnel through the Pyrénées, usually open year round. Tunnel closed at night and subject to weather conditions.

Bosruck (A9 Pyhrn Autobahn), Austria*

This road tunnel is 5.5km long and runs between Spital am Pyhrn and Selzthal, to the east of the Pyhrn Pass. It forms part of the Pyhrn Autobahn between Linz and Graz.

Rates (in AS)

Motorcycle	60
Car, minibus (up to 9 seats)	70
Caravan or trailer	30

Cadi, Spain

The 5km-long tunnel between Bellver de Cerdanya and Bagá on the C1411, to the west of the Tosas Pass.

Rates (in Ptas) (correct October 1997)

motorcycle, car, car and 2 wheeled trailers, minibus	1260 Ptas

Frejus, France/Italy

The tunnel between Modane and Bardonecchia is 12.8km long and open all year.
Tolls similar to the Mont Blanc tunnel. Sidelights must be used. Speed limits: min 60kph – max 80kph.

Gleinalm (A9 Pyhrn autobahn), Austria*

The road tunnel between St Michael and Friesach, near Graz, is 8.3km long and forms part of the A9 road from Linz to Slovenia.

Rates (in AS)

motorcycle	100
car, minibus (up to 9 seats)	110
caravan or trailer	30

Great St Bernard, Switzerland/Italy

The road tunnel between Bourg St Pierre and Aosta (Etroubles) is 6km long.
From both sides there are modern approach roads with wide curves, gradual inclines and permanent protection against snow, ensuring easy access all year.
Swiss and Italian frontier posts are on the Swiss side and there is a money exchange office, restaurant, snack bar, petrol station and parking at each entrance to the tunnel.

Rates (in Sw F) (subject to increase in 1999)

motorcycle	15
car (according to wheelbase)	27
car with caravan or trailer	27
motor caravan	56.50

Karawanken, Austria/Slovenia

This road tunnel links Austria with Slovenia between St Jakob and Jesenice.

Rates (in AS)

motorcycle	90
car (not exceeding1.3m in height)	90
car with caravan or trailer	135
motor caravan	135

Katschberg, Austria*

A two-lane carriageway 5.4km long forming part of the motorway between Salzburg and Carinthia (Tauern autobahn).

Rates (in AS)

motorcycle	50
car	70
caravan or trailer	20

Lötschberg, Switzerland

Vehicles are transported through the Lötschberg Tunnel between Kandersteg and Goppenstein. Service daily 0605–2305 (leaving every 30 minutes).

Rates (in Sw F)

motorcycle, baggage trailer	16
car, caravan, motorcaravan (per unit)	25
minibus (10–19 seats)	36

Mont Blanc, France/Italy

Tunnel between Chamonix and Entrèves,11.6km long, at an altitude of 1370m. Customs at the Italian end. Side and rear lights must be used.

Rates (in FF)

motorcycle	95
car (according to wheelbase)	95-188
car with caravan or trailer	188

Munt La Schera, Switzerland/Italy

This road tunnel links Zernez and Livigno in Italy. The tunnel is closed between 2000 hours and 0800 hours. The maximum height is 3.60m and the maximum width is 2.50m.

Rates (in Sw F)

motorcycle	8
car	12
caravan	16

Netherlands

Tolls in Florins, on the following:

Kiltunnel (Dordecht–Hoekse)

motorcycle	3.50
car (acc. to height at front axle)	3.50/10.00

Puymorens, France

On the N20 east of Andorra between Ax-les-Thermes and Latour.

Rates (in FF)

motorcycle	19
car	32

Radstadter Tauern, Austria

The road tunnel is 6.5km long (parallel to the Tauern railway tunnel) on the Salzburg–Carinthia route.

Tolls as for the Katschberg tunnel.

St Gotthard, Switzerland

The two-lane road tunnel is 16.3km long running under the Gotthard Pass from Göschenen to Airolo.

Part of the national motorway network, so display the special vignette.

St Marie aux Mines, France

The 13km road tunnel in the Vosges region is located to the north-west of Colmar between St. Die and Sélestat (N159/N59).

Rates (in FF)

motorcycle	11
car	19
car with caravan or trailer	38

San Bernardino, Switzerland

The 6.6km road tunnel runs parallel to the Pass on the N13.

Part of the national motorway network, the special vignette must be displayed.

Tauern, Austria

Up to 47 trains a day convey vehicles between Bockstein and Mallnitz.

Passengers may travel in closed cars, but only drivers in lorries and coaches. Load vehicles 30 mins before departure. The Austrian Federal Railways issue a timetable.

Rates (in AS) (correct for 1998)

motorcycle	100
car, summer (1/5–31/10)	190
caravan or trailer	80

Mountain passes

The major mountain passes are listed by country and by road classification within each country. The term 'intermittent closure' refers to regular snow clearance which may take two or three days. All Swiss passes listed have emergency telephones (for mechanical, police or medical help and free of charge) at two-mile intervals. Emergency water supplies are usually available. The Automobile Club de Suisse and the Touring Club de Suisse have a Road Assistance Service in the Alpine regions. RAC strongly recommends against driving over mountain passes at night and would advise inexperienced drivers to avoid mountain passes or to drive with extreme care. For details of other mountain passes please contact RAC Travel Information.

Key to abbreviations

Altr	alternative
Ch	winter snow chains
Min rad	minimum radius
Mod	moderate/ly
N	North
nec	necessary
No	prohibited by law
NR	not recommended
Oc	occasionally
Pic	picturesque
S	South
Tr	treacherous
u/c	unclassified road

Road number and road (borders) Name of Pass and height (in metres)	Min width (ft)	Max grad	Cond. in winter	Rec. caravans	Remarks
ANDORRA					
N2 L'Hospitalet to Andorra ENVALIRA 2407	20	1:8	Closed Nov-Apr	Yes*	*Extra care required. Good snow clearance, but can be closed after a heavy fall. Max height of vehicles 11'6. Highest pass in Pyrénées
AUSTRIA					
B99 Spittal to Radstadt KATSCHBERG 1641	20	1:5	Usually open	No*	Fairly difficult. Light traffic. *Altr motorway tunnel (toll).
B107 Bruck to Lienz GROSSGLOCKNER 2505	16	1:8	Closed late Oct–May	No*	Toll. *Only powerful caravan units, preferably S-N. Hairpin bends, excep. views. Tunnel at summit.
138 Windischgarsten to Liezen PYHRN 945	13	1:10	Usually open	Yes	Hairpins. Altr road tunnel (toll).
B145 Bad Ischl to Bad Aussee POTSCHEN 972	23	1:11	Usually open	Yes	Views of the Dachstein. Mod to heavy traffic.
B161 Kitzbühel to Mittersill THURN 1274	16	1:12	Usually open	Yes	Scenic. Mod to heavy traffic.
B182/SS12 Innsbruck to Bolzano (Austria–Italy) BRENNER 1374	20	1:7	Usually open	No*	Pic. Lowest, busiest transalpine pass. Ch sometimes. Pass is closed to vehicles towing.
B197 Feldkirch to Innsbruck ARLBERG 1793	20	1:7.5	Closed Dec–Apr	No*	Pic. Easy, heavy traffic. *Closed to vehicles towing (toll).

Road number and road (borders) Name of Pass and height (in metres)	Min width (ft)	Max grad	Cond. in winter	Rec. caravans	Remarks
B314 Imst to Reutte FERN 1210	20	1:10	Usually open	Yes	Easy pass. Heavy traffic. Extra care required after rain.
B315/SS40 Landeck to Malles (Austria–Italy) RESIA 1504	20	1:10	Usually open	Yes	Mod to heavy traffic. Pic altr to the Brenner Pass.
FRANCE					
N5 Morez to Genève FAUCILLE 1323	16	1:10	Usually open	No*	*Experience necessary. Altr via Nyon–Genève. View of Mt Blanc.
N6 Chambéry to Torino MT CENIS 2083	16	1:8	Closed early Nov–mid May	Yes	Heavy summer traffic, easy. Poor surface. Altr road tunnel (toll).
N20 Toulouse to Bourg-Madame PUYMORENS 1915	18	1:10	Closed Nov–Apr	Yes	Altr rail tunnel.(toll)* Not suitable for night driving. Max height 11'6.
N75 Grenoble to Sisteron CROIX-HAUTE 1176	18	1:14	Usually open	Yes	Hairpin bends. Open to all vehicles.
N85 Grenoble to Gap (Route des Alpes) BAYARD 1248	20	1:7	Usually open	No*	Easy, steep S side and hairpins. *Just negotiable for caravans N-S.
N90/SS26 Bourg-St-Maurice to Aosta PETIT ST BERNARD 2188	16	1:12	Closed mid-Oct–mid June	No	Light traffic. Pic. No vehicles over 15t. Unguarded edges at summit Unguarded edges. NR buses.
N91 Briançon to Vizille LAUTARET/ALTARETO 2058	14	1:8	Closed Dec–Mar	Yes	Heavy summer traffic. Magnificent scenery.
N94/SS24 Briançon to Torino (France–Italy) MONTGENEVRE 1850	16	1:11	Usually open	Yes	Open all year. Altr Mt Cenis. Heavy traffic. Pic. Ch.
N204/SS20 La Giandola to Borgo San Dalmazzo (France–Italy) COL DE TENDE 1321	18	1:11	Usually open	Yes*	Summer traffic. Tunnel summit. Hairpin bends. *No caravans in winter. Closed 2100–0600 hrs.
ITALY					
SS12/B182 Bolzano to Innsbruck (Italy–Austria) BRENNER 1374	20	1:7	Usually open	No*	Pic. Lowest, busiest transalpine pass, closed to vehicles towing.
SS20/N204 Borgo San Dalmazzo to La Giandola COL DE TENDE 1321	18	1:11	Usually open	Yes*	Summer traffic. Tunnel at summit. Hairp. bends. *No caravans winter.
SS24/N94 Torino to Briançon (Italy–France) MONTGENEVRE 1850	16	1:11	Usually open	Yes	Open all year. Altr Mt Cenis. Heavy traffic. Pic. Ch.
SS26/N90 Aosta to Bourg-St-Maurice PETIT ST BERNARD 2188	16	1:12	Closed mid-Oct–mid June	No	Light traffic. Pic. No vehicles over 15 t. Unguarded edges at summit.
SS27/A21 Aosta to Martigny (Italy–Switzerland) GREAT ST BERNARD 2473	16	1:10	Closed Oct–June	No*	*Closed to vehicles towing. Ch required on approach roads, not permitted through tunnel.
SS36 Chiavenna to Splügen (Italy–Switzerland) SPLUGEN 2113	10	1:7.5	Closed early Nov–June	No	Pic. Many hairpins, not well guarded. Max height of vehicles 9'2. Max width 7'6.
SS38 Bormio to Spondigna STELVIO 2757	13	1:8	Closed Oct-late June	No	Many hairpins, very scenic. No vehicles over 30ft in length.
SS40/B315 Malles to Landeck (Italy–Austria) RESIA 1504	20	1:10	Usually open	Yes	Mod to heavy traffic. Pic Altr to the Brenner Pass.

Road number and road (borders) / Name of Pass and height (in metres)	Min width (ft)	Max grad	Cond. in winter	Rec. caravans	Remarks
SPAIN					
N152 Barcelona to Puigcerdà TOSAS 1800	16	1:10	Usually open	Yes*	Sharp bends, unguarded edges. *Negotiable for caravans with care.
N240 Pamplona to Donostia/San Sebastián AZPIROZ 616	19	1:10	Usually open	Yes	Double bends. Min radius bends 42'.
N330/N134 Huesca to Pau SOMPORT 1632	12	1:10	Usually open	Yes	Usual route across Pyrénées. Narrow and unguarded in parts.
C135 Pamplona to St-Jean-Pied-de-Port IBANETA 1057	13	1:10	Usually open	Yes*	Pic. *Drive with care.
SWITZERLAND					
N2 Andermatt to Bellinzona ST GOTTHARD 2108	20	1:10	Closed mid Oct–early June	Yes*	No vehicles over 8'2½ wide or 11'9 high. Many hairpins and heavy summer traffic.
N8 (N4) Meiringen to Lucerne BRUNIG 1007	20	1:12	Usually open	Yes	No vehicles over 8'2½" wide. Ch sometimes. Traffic at weekends.
N9 Brig to Domodossola SIMPLON 2005	23	1:9	Closed Nov–Apr	Yes	Max width 8'2". An easy reconstructed road.
N13 Chur to Bellinzona SAN BERNARDINO 2006	3	1:10	Closed Oct–late June	No*	Easy approach roads, but narrow, winding summit. Max width 7'6.
A3 Tiefencastel to Silvaplana JULIER 2284	13	1:7.5	Usually open	Yes*	*Easier N-S. Max width 8'2½. Altr rail tunnel Tiefencastelsamedan.
A3 Chiavenna to Silvaplana MALOJA 1815	13	1:11	Usually open	Yes*	Hairpin bends on descent. No trailers. Max width 8'2½.
A6 Gletsch to Innertkirchen GRIMSEL 2165	16	1:10	Closed mid Oct–late June	No	Max width 7'6. Hairpins, seasonal traffic. Max weight trailers 2½t.
A19 Andermatt to Brig FURKA 2431	13	1:10	Closed Oct–June	No	Seasonal traffic. No vehicles over 7'6 wide. Many hairpin bends.
A21/SS27 Martigny to Aosta GREAT ST BERNARD 2473	16	1:10	Closed Oct–June	No*	*Closed to vehicles towing. Fairly easy – care required over summit.
(SS36) Splügen to Chiavenna (Switzerland–Italy) SPLUGEN 2113	10	1:7.5	Closed early Nov–June	No	Pic. Many hairpin bends, not well guarded. Max height of vehicles 9'2. Max width of vehicles 7'6.

Customs allowances

	Duty Paid Goods obtained duty and tax paid in the EU
Cigarettes, or	800
Cigarillos, or	400
Cigars, or	200
Tobacco	1 kg
Still table wine	* see below
Spirits, strong liqeurs over 22% volume, or	10 litres
Fortified or sparkling wine, other liqeurs	* 20 litres of fortified wine, or 90 litres of wine (of which no more than 60 litres of sparkling wine)
Perfume	no limit
Toilet water	no limit
All other goods including gifts	no limit, except for the beer allowance, which is increased to 110 litres

Duty-paid goods

Provided they are for your personal use, there is no further tax to be paid on goods you have obtained duty and tax paid in the European Union. Personal use includes gifts. Member states still reserve the right to check that products are for personal use only, and not for resale purposes. For this reason, the EU has set guide levels, as shown above, and if you bring more than the amounts in the guide levels you are required to show that the goods are for your own personal use.

Travelling within the EU

If you are travelling to the UK directly from another EU country, you do not need to go through a red or green channel, and you do not need to make any declaration to Customs. However, selective checks will still be carried out by Customs to detect prohibited goods.

Entering the UK

You may have valuable items such as cameras, radios or watches which were bought into the UK, or which have been bought through Customs before and any Customs charges paid. It is a good idea to carry receipts for these items where possible, so that they can be checked by a Customs officer if necessary.
If you are entering the UK in a vehicle, it is important that everyone travelling with you knows what goods are prohibited or restricted. If goods are smuggled in a car, the car may be confiscated. Never carry anything into the UK for someone else. No-one under the age of 17 is entitled to tobacco or drink allowances.

Prohibited and restricted goods

In order to protect health and the environment, certain goods cannot be freely imported. The main items are as follows and further information can be obtained by contacting the government body indicated:

Animals, birds and reptiles

The importation of most species, whether alive or dead (eg stuffed), and many items derived from protected species, eg fur skins, ivory, reptile leather and goods made from them, is restricted. Such items can be imported only if you have prior authority (eg a licence) to import them.

Counterfeit or 'copy' goods

Goods bearing a false indication of their origin and goods in breach of UK copyright are prohibited and must not be brought into the UK.

Drugs

Do not import controlled drugs, eg heroin, cocaine, cannabis, amphetamines and LSD. If you require drugs for medical reasons, further information can be obtained from: The Home Office Drugs Branch, 50 Queen Anne's Gate, London SW1H 9AT.

Endangered species

The Department of the Environment operates controls on the import of endangered species. Enquiries should be made to DoE, Endangered Species Branch, Tollgate House, Houlton Street, Bristol BS2 9DJ, Tel: 0117-987 8202.

Firearms and ammunition

Firearms and ammunition (including gas pistols, gas canisters, electric shock batons and similar weapons) are restricted and can only be imported if you have prior authority (eg a licence) to import them. Explosives (including fireworks) are banned completely.

Foodstuffs

The importation of meat, poultry and their products including ham, bacon, sausage, pâté, eggs, milk and cream is restricted.
You are allowed 1kg of meat per person as long as it is fully cooked and in airtight containers. Further information from: Ministry of Agriculture, Fisheries and Food, Tel: 0181 330 4411.

Pets

Cats, dogs and other mammals must not be brought into the UK unless a British import licence (rabies) has previously been issued. A period of six months quarantine is required. All live birds also require an import licence.

Plants and plant produce

To safeguard against pests and diseases, certain plants and plant produce are prohibited. Others are restricted and must be certified as healthy by the exporting country. You do not, however, need these certificates if the plant material your bring back is:
– in your personal baggage
– for your own use and not for trade or business
– free from signs of pests and diseases.
These conditions apply in all cases, but concessions may vary depending on the country you are returning from.
If you are returning from a country inside the European Community (EC) you may bring back any plant material, providing it was grown in the EC.
If you are returning from a non-EC country and the plant material is restricted you may bring back no more than:
– 2kg of fruit and
– a single bouquet of cut flowers and foliage and
– five retail packages of seeds (not potatoes).
From Euro-Mediterranean countries (these include Algeria, the Canary Island, Cyprus, Egypt, Israel, Jordan, Lebanon, Libya, Malta, Morocco, Norway, Switzerland, Syria, Tunisia and Turkey).
In addition to the non-EC concession you may bring back no more than:
– five plants and
– 2kg of bulbs, corms, tubers (not potatoes) and rhizomes.
No potatoes may be imported from any non-EC country under these concessions.
Full details of what you can and cannot bring back into Britain are available from Plant Health Division, Ministry of Agriculture, Fisheries and Food, Foss House, 1-2 Pearholme Green, Kings Pool, York YO1 2PX. Tel: 01904 455191.

Other prohibited goods

These include offensive weapons such as flick knives, butterfly knives, knuckledusters, swordsticks, and some martial arts weapons; counterfeit currency; radio transmitters and cordless telephones not approved for use in the UK; obscene books, videos etc; horror comics; anglers' lead weights.